Website: https://www.paulette-marie-reymond.com
Email: contact@paulette-marie-reymond.com

Translation: Translingua AG
https://www.translingua.ch

Cover design: Katja Jost
https://www.katjajost.ch

Cover photo: Paulette Marie Reymond, Karnak, Egypt

Print and distribution: Amazon KDP

ISBN paperback: 9798647420534

Also available as a Kindle eBook.

Harmonisation of the Polarities

***

Messages from Sekhmet

channelled by Paulette Marie Reymond

About the Author

 Paulette Marie Reymond lives in Switzerland. She has two adult daughters. For 30 years, she has been working as a Channel with the Spiritual Hierarchy of Earth, the Archangels, high cosmic entities and cosmic siblings. She wants to support Earth and her people in this time of ascension to a new octave of being.

Website: https://www.paulette-marie-reymond.com

En souvenir de Rosalie et Charly.

Acknowledgement

While on the search for my own self, I became aware of the presence of Mother Sekhmet in the early 1990s. Her companionship is a common theme throughout my life. She called me, among other things, to Karnak in Egypt, where her energy touched me deeply in her temple. I felt at home again there for the first time in a long time.

Thank you, dear Mother Sekhmet, for the sign you gave me in Karnak, for your love, your patience, and your commitment. I am deeply honoured to pass on your messages to humankind.

In deep love,
Paulette Marie Reymond

Table of contents

Sekhmet

From the beginning, I have been connected to Earth and her people in love. I have the task of bringing Light into the dark for mankind, to point them on the way of their evolutionary path, and to render my support. For this reason, many civilisations have revered me as a goddess. As the first mother of the solar mastery, my energy has helped bring about evolution on this planet. Right now, you are facing a quantum leap on the path of Light. These messages are part of my dedication to mankind, for the resurrection of humans as multidimensional beings of Light. Light is the origin, and the destiny, of all of us. In this Light, we are all connected for eternity. Let the divine Light radiate inside you and shine in its glory. Recognise yourselves for who you truly are, and create New Earth. Penetrate into new realities, embrace what is past and let it go.

Let Light and Love flow once again, and enjoy your lives on this wonderful planet Earth.

Light and Love are the basis for all that exists and realisation of our existence. Embedded in All-That-Is, we continue on together into the Light. Origin and destiny merge in the Now, manifesting New Earth, your home.

Praised be mankind for its courage and perseverance, and praised be our creator god, our creator goddess, which rest in us all.

Sekhmet

Introduction

The Fifth-Dimensional quality of harmonisation of the polarities is a novelty for the residents of Earth. It will cause some changes to your conduct, which you have yet to learn and integrate. However, this will lead mankind to the galactic civilisations and accelerate its integration into those. Harmonisation of polarities affects several aspects of your life on Earth. However, I would like to specifically dedicate and commit myself to harmonisation of the female and male principles. It is particularly close to my heart, since these polarities are gaping apart vastly in many places on Earth, causing great pain and suffering. Additionally, a great potential of talents is left unused, which is now becoming vital. The female potential in particular is invaluable for this ascension into the Fifth Dimension. It will bring mankind a new, female view of things and their implementation. By female potential, I not only mean that of women, but also that of men who wish to accept and actively practice their female aspects. The female talents I speak of are intuition, sensitivity, creativity, dedication, contact with Earth, and so on. This book will, therefore, go more deeply into these areas of potential, explain them, and give you courage to study those polarities and to find a consensus. That consensus happens in every individual, no matter their gender. It is, first and foremost, inner work that will thereafter manifest outwards, in order to severely change your societies. Religious and societal manipulations will have to be recognised and transformed. There is a lot of fundamental work ahead of you. You will have to go deep inside you, to study your inclinations and wishes, and to transform them, where necessary, in order to enable human societies to fully utilise their true potentials and to be reborn into a higher dimension in harmony with Mother Earth. The humans ready for this will develop this ascension together with Earth.

The galactic civilisations are waiting for you with great joy. The current time of ascension on Earth will give you great experience in how a society can transform from a strongly polarised Third- and Fourth-Dimensional quality into a Fifth-Dimensional one. The time ahead of you will not be easy. Yet, everyone will feel the urge towards harmonisation inside themselves. Whether to give in to that search and transformation is a decision every individual must make on their own. Everyone bears full responsibility for themselves, and must be able to rely on themselves for their decisions. Manipulation will be uncovered, and interrelations will become clear. The new clarity that is now brought by this increasing energy will cause certain living situations to collapse and give way to new, cooperative models. The increase of energy will support that process. However, reactionary forces are unlikely to give up their privilege freely. It will, therefore, be a difficult project at first. The Fifth-Dimensional quality will prevail step by step, however, and enable mankind to fully unfold itself.

Historical Context

A very long time ago, when the first humans settled on Lemuria, the polarities were not yet gaping apart. The residents of Lemuria at the time were messengers from the stars, aiming to help Earth reach a higher dimension with their cosmic love. That process continues to this day. Many Lemurians are incarnated today, when they can finally harvest what they have sown. A long period has passed in Earthly time, but it is a natural time span in cosmic terms. Many incarnations were necessary, as was the submersion in very dark times. This had to happen in order to get to know the entire range of energies here on Earth before permitting ascension into a higher dimension. The polarities started drifting apart severely in this process, no matter if societies were matriarchal or patriarchal. Now, however, the time of harmonisation has come, where both energies meet at the centre. There, a joint expression must be found in order to continue on the next step of human evolution.

Societies in some regions of Earth have been able to develop farther than others. At the moment, Earth is experiencing great discrepancies between female and male energies. They should, must, and will slowly balance themselves out. The ascension of the residents of Earth is not limited to some elitist class, but will encompass all humans willing to take responsibility for themselves, their society, and Earth. Earth will be accepted by the galactic civilisations as a whole. Additionally, the increase of energy will no longer permit discrimination of parts of the population. This energy increase will awaken people and transform their societies. You will be amazed at the changes that are about to happen soon. These are changes you would never have dared dream of before. Of course, polarity will increase first. It has never been easy to let go of power. Find the new energies in that sad game, however, and be confident that consensus will follow. That process will be a great challenge for mankind. It will cut right through your very intimate family cells. Actually, that is a place of love. Love in all its facets will be tested. It will lead to rebirth in many places. There will be a deeply pervasive process, a process that will teach you love and cooperation. What has manifested in your families and partnerships greatly influences your societies, religions, and nations. That process will not happen on the outside, but inside every individual, influencing the whole.

Your star siblings support that process. Ask them for help to allow them more active commitment. They have a close eye on this process of harmonisation. You are not alone in your transformation phase. They are with you, just as they have always been, and as they are always going to be. They are not separate from you. We are all one in the ONE. You had to persevere through all the dark processes. Now, however, you are ready to pass through the Fifth-Dimensional gate. Welcome home!

The times in which you are now living on Earth are characterised by great upheavals. They are upheavals that will pervasively change your private, social, and national lives. These changes started several years ago, unnoticed by some, drastic for others. Be assured, dear residents of Earth, that this is part of your transformation, the renewal of the circumstances of life in all their facets. Many may find it exceedingly difficult to recognise that their habits, their rituals, and their established networks are dissolving. Resisting this change, clinging to old conditions, will cost you a lot of energy and many detours. Instead, use that energy to accept the new realities, in order to find your own path in this apparent chaos. That path may fit and support you better. The strengthened energies that are now being sent to Earth will guide and assist you. Turn far inwards and question your wishes and talents. Are they supporting your new lives in unity with the whole? Egotistical goals that do not consider the unity have little chance of survival. New humans will be committed to the whole as a resident of Earth, helping mankind master the octave jump into the Fifth Dimension. This time of transition and the onset of the new era will lead to an abundance of creative changes. Every individual who is willing to set out on this path will achieve fulfilment. It is the path of freedom in harmony with responsibility and love for the whole. These statements will come true step by step now, helping mankind as a whole solve the many present problems and build new, creative structures. This time on Earth is truly a new birth, not only for Mother Earth, but also for her humans. Being part of this process now is an extraordinary grace and opportunity. Even though it may be hard at times, never forget that aspect. It will give you courage, confidence, and strength to accept what is new and to put it into practice.

Great, old souls are currently incarnated on Earth. They are loving Lemurians who now await the harvest of their seed, and who initiate, monitor, and support the last growth spurts. Mankind receives plenty of spiritual help now. Thanks to the great growth of consciousness, they are finally able to accept and understand that help after all the years of deprivation. This spiritual help does not come to you from the outside. We were never separate. Only your limited perception kept you from seeing. This time of the thick veil that kept us apart is coming to an end. The increased energy will cause the veil to gradually dissipate, letting you perceive the beings who support you. I would like to particularly awaken the entities of Earth in you. They are your elves, your gnomes, your devas, etc. Rely in their support. They belong to you, and to your life on Earth. They will provide valuable support to you in interaction with Mother Earth, with whom you are living in symbiosis. Your path from here on can only be possible with Earth, Gaia, or Terra, no matter what you call her. Be deeply aware of this fact. It will change your interaction with her drastically. Phrases like "exploitation of Earth", "subdue the Earth", etc. will dissolve, to be replaced by respect for her. Where would you go if Earth no longer carried you? It is a fundamental question that you have to face, also in light of the coming generations that you have brought to life. Your considerations require every individual to take responsibility. That responsibility is now about to change mankind and the whole pervasively. Do not think that you can stay apart from this. It is not something that only concerns others. This is a global process that involves all of mankind.

The female qualities are outstanding for comprehending and deepening access to Mother Earth. After all, menstruation and birth connects women to, and familiarises them with, the rhythms of Earth. They feel them in their bodies. Access to these rhythms must be felt. It cannot be understood by reason. Women have had this potential since the ancient times. Do not let those talents go. It is an invaluable treasure for mankind to have this potential be part of human societies in its entirety. The symbiosis with Gaia can then be experienced and lived consciously. It is a connection of the goddesses for the good of all life in the Here-and-Now and in the cosmos alike.

Changes of all kinds will continue to accompany you for a while to come. Being ready for this will make your lives easier. Try living in flow with the innovations, and to creatively participate in changes in your private lives and your work. The great economic, social, and religious changes that will dominate Earth in the next few years will give you a new understanding of the interrelations on Earth and in the cosmos. It's a process of slowly growing into new areas of knowledge, new forms of conduct, new opinions of the whole. This revolution will change humans pervasively, making them compatible with the galactic civilisations. Galactic contacts will become the most natural thing in the world for humans, whose self-worth will then be equal to that of alien societies. Exchange can then happen among partners, to nurture all parties and let them teach each other.

The growth of human consciousness will now culminate in renewal or rebirth in a higher octave. The learning processes will happen in a more highly and quickly vibrating energy, which will greatly accelerate the evolution of mankind. Earth is now ready to take her conscious place in the cosmic dance and to make her contribution.

Rejoice, dear citizens of Earth, that you have finally reached the maturity to take cosmic action. You will certainly enjoy your star siblings' respect. They have closely observed and supported your evolution after all.

New Frames of Understanding

The solar emanations are now bringing you information that will re-programme and complete your genetic code. Great change is happening. It will, however, help you better handle the new conditions by expanding your capacity for thought. The quality of your hearts will also develop on a higher level now, enabling you to tackle positive human progress. A new understanding of things will be necessary to balance out your gaping male/female polarity. You will have to develop part of this understanding on your own, though you will receive lots of energetic help from the cosmos, e.g. from solar information that penetrate you and Earth, as well as the energetic help of your star siblings. Do not forget that you are, in the end, also star seed. Your memory will slowly awaken now. You will remember your roots and know why you have chosen Earth as the place of your incarnation. Your task of bringing the code of paradise onto Earth is nearly complete. Your mission will soon be fulfilled. You have done great work through your many life cycles, enabling mankind to ascend onto the higher vibrational octave together with Earth. The code of paradise is present in every human. The accelerated solar energy is now decoding it. This will enable many changes that are still impossible, or at least exceedingly difficult, now. Trust in yourselves, and watch the changes in the conduct of those your kin and neighbours. You will see that the new energetic alignment is manifesting and that conditions are changing.

The code of paradise is cosmic Love itself, manifesting on Earth now. Those following Christian religions call it the awareness of Christ. Southern and Meso-American philosophies call it the return of the Feathered Serpent, the return of Quetzalcoatl or Kukulkan. For the Jews, it will be the long-expected Messiah. Everyone will absorb that energy of Love, develop it, and spread it on. Earth is about to become what she has always been: paradise, with the people being aware of their divinity in unity. The separation of All-That-Is will be a thing of the past, of the Third and Fourth Dimensions.

Even though some changes still need to happen, the goal is promising. It will give you courage and confidence to master the last obstacles and to create new paradigms for your lives together. You are no longer fighting alone. You are now a great army of Light-filled humans returning to paradise.

By these changes, Earth and her humans are given the opportunity to actively participate in the galactic meetings of the forces of Light and to make their contribution.

Inner and Outer Changes

The changes that are now happening in your minds, your bodies, your societies and nations also act on Earth and nature. These processes allow you to develop a global understanding of the pending issues. You will develop the laws for the good of Earth and mankind in full responsibility. Weaker societies will be supported by stronger ones. Only together can you solve the pending issues and thereby operate an international policy that considers everyone. The female forces will play a great role in this process and receive the opportunity to fully engage, not only in the scope of families but on a planetary scope. Limitation of the female forces to the family domain will be broken. This will lead to great changes in particular in patriarchal societies. Women's self-worth will increase, as is urgently required for the future. In some areas, suppression and force have made them develop a stronger feeling for Mother Earth and her rhythms. That potential is available to everyone. You would be well advised to involve those women in your processes as advisors. The climate issues of Earth should not be tackled with a strictly scientific approach, but relying on the contribution of indigenous populations and women. Listen to the long tradition of the indigenous peoples, and their connection to Earth. You will be amazed to see how they can contribute to mankind. They will teach you how the Earth's population should handle its planet – its home. This will provide you with approaches for great changes to your way of thinking and acting, and allow you to correct issues.

With delays, and yet within the deadline set, you will renew your communities and raise them to a new level. Trust in this process. Do not be discouraged, even if the barriers you encounter are frustrating for you. Know that you will be victorious in the end. You will prevail over egotism and narrow-mindedness. Centuries-old traditions and rituals are difficult to change. After all, such changes require an increase of consciousness. This increase of consciousness of mankind continues. It is unstoppable, now more quickly, now more slowly. You and your societies must integrate this new accelerated energy down to the very base in order to achieve sustainable change without any great battles. Watch the details change more and more. The snowball principle will take care of the rest. The societies of Earth will renew, and the female and male principles will solve the problems faced in Earth creatively together. There is much to do to ensure balance in your cohabitation, and to create a society that focuses on the needs of Earth as a whole.

Only as global citizens of Earth will you have access to the galactic civilisations. Discrimination of the North-South-East-West-axes or racial affiliation will dissolve. You are all residents of Earth! That is truly a very special thing, isn't it? Territorial characteristics and specialisations will become part of all your goals for the good of everyone. Unimagined treasures will disclose themselves to you. Some of these are talents that are still unaccessed now. The feeling of community will strengthen you and you will notice that you are actually all one. There is no separation between you, mankind, and Earth. This deep understanding will help you solve issues in a holistic manner, and extra-terrestrial contact will be the most natural thing in the world.

The process that I have pointed out to you is partially still ahead of you. However, you have been on this path for a while. The current acceleration of energy will let you progress more quickly. Walk it with confidence and courage. You have the strength you need, and the support of your cosmic siblings is certain.

Sexuality

The farther the polarities of the male and female are gaping apart, the larger the energetic tension between those poles. Sexuality is of great importance on Earth. Because of this, it has been cast into laws, catalogued, demonised, or declared non-existent in all of your religions. Sexuality serves biological further development of the human species! That is why it was considered a necessary evil in many places. Women who manifest the fruit of sexuality were, and still are, humiliated, abused, and considered second-class. They are, and were, considered the sole perpetrators of sexual lust by the male aspect. Dark times with these issues are behind you. However, this is still present in many patriarchal societies.

The current increase of energy on Earth will render these issues less severe, as the male and female polarity approach harmonisation. That means that polar tension will be harmonised step by step. Men and women will become more relaxed and their coexistence will be improved. Men and women will learn to understand each other as partners, both in the family and in society.

Association with one gender or the other will increasingly move into the background, giving way to models of partnership.

Harmonious, lust-filled sexuality will take place between partners. Lust-filled sexuality is an important tool of mankind to provide their physical and mental balance. It can even serve the personal spiritual path and advance humans far in their consciousness.

The farther mankind moves into the Fifth Dimension, the more they will develop towards androgyny. Do not imagine the development towards androgyny in the Fifth Dimension as being sexless. You will remain in the bodies of your sex that you chose at birth, with all of its specific benefits and attributes. However, sexual energy will lose its tension field. You will no longer be subject to your libido, but able to decide on your own whether you want to exercise your sexuality with a partner or not. Sexuality will bring you close to your partner and to yourself. You will be able to climb into ecstatic heights together, carried by this lust-filled energy. It is a wonderful tool for your development, while also serving to preserve mankind.

Misunderstood sexuality has caused great pain and suffering for mankind, and in particular for woman. Those traumas are now healed. Women will once again receive their due position in society, where they will work for the good of the greater whole.

The attraction between the sexes will always exist. The minus and plus poles will not dissolve. You will preserve your polarity, but it will be harmonised. That will lead to you finding a consensus for many of the issues that are still predominant today. Respect for each other will be more strongly present in your relationships. Couples will support each other and guide and educate their children accordingly. The fight between the sexes is nearing its end. These new energies are already flowing into your relationships, starting to undermine social structures. Societal structures will have to adjust to new humanity and its needs.

Harmonisation of the field of tension of the female and male polarity will free up a lot of energy and time for activities and tasks. That energy will be of great help to you for rebuilding your societies. Rather than losing anything, you will gain something from this! You may still be sceptical today, but that process is already in the course of gradually coming into being. Accept this new energy. It will liberate you. Men and women of this Earth: become fully aware of your responsibility as humans. You are, first and foremost, humans after all – merely living in different bodies!

Intimacy between Genders

We have talked about sexuality already, but we did not mention the love that connects the sexes. Sexuality can take place without mutual love. That was even rather common. As the energy increase processes, however, mutual love between sexual partners will become more and more important, and even necessary, depending on the state of consciousness of those involved. Sexuality and intimacy gives love between the partners a very special importance. Love comes in many facets. Erotic love enables its many facets to integrate in the body, and to reach every single cell. They can harmonise and nurture bodies. This asset will no longer be abused, but will receive its unique status in a couple's relationship. Of course, this quality has been exercised by many couples for a long time. Now, however, mankind as a whole will become aware of it and accept it as a divine gift. The physical aspects belong to you just as the spiritual ones do. You are a whole. No part of you is inferior. Man as a whole will now move forward into the Light. Physicality should be given more attention now. You are surely familiar with the phrase: A healthy soul resides in a healthy body! The soul can only manifest through your bodies. Question your ailments, to enable you to heal them on a higher level. Your bodies will no longer need to suffer any symptoms. This approach to healing is rather new for you, but it will become more and more established in the near future, giving way to an integrated claim to healing. Symptoms will still be treated, but this will happen in an integrated context.

You are the products of many incarnations on Earth. You have experienced lots of joy, but also lots of trauma. All of that is stored in your bodies. It is now released for transformation with the accelerated energy. Look at the processes that are happening and let go of old patterns and blocks to move on more freely into the higher vibrational octave. Blocks manifest not only on the physical level. They can also interfere with and destroy your romantic and other relationships of all kinds. Look behind the scenes of events. Try to achieve your own consensus or harmonisation that you need to be liberated for your further path.

The current times are full of transformations in all human areas. Trust in this new energy, though surely it is not always easy. It will guide you where you need to be. Move with the flow. Do not try to cling to the old and outdated. It will be impossible, while also depleting you of energy and exhausting you. Letting go is the great theme of this time, in order to continue on under your own responsibility, with courage and joy. Joy and fun are your companions. Try seeing the humorous side in all of it. The new energy is full of this! Transformation does not mean suffering and depression. It is a liberation that will guide you to become the new humans that you have truly been for eons. You will become divine, co-creating beings, residents of this paradise that is Earth.

The many relationship problems that couples have today are strongly caused by the accelerated energies. On the one hand, there is the process of individuation. Everyone becomes aware of their wishes in life and would, of course, like to be able to practice them. As an individual, that would surely be possible. In a relationship in which one has sworn mutual life-long commitment, however, things will get difficult when one or both partners notice over time that they cannot live fulfilled lives of their own. Increasing consciousness will not be integrated by all people at the same time. That makes discrepancies unavoidable. People will have to find new relationship structures. They are already in the process of creating them anew. Laws must, by necessity, adjust to this new situation, and support humans in their right to their own, fulfilled lives. Societies will adjust to new man. Old paradigms have become obsolete! The new relationships will be based on mutual love while it carries both parties. Love doesn't really need laws. The economical concepts developed from relationships between couples are what may require laws. Everyone will enter into relationships in full individual responsibility in future, bearing the corresponding consequences for themselves and for their relationships.

In order to take this step into full responsibility, every human must strive to centre themselves. Of course, your everyday lives will not allow you to always be centred. However, you should try to develop your connection to yourselves. Instead of looking for a solution for your problems on the outside, become familiar with yourselves and your inside. You will encounter unexpected treasures and new talents that disclose themselves. You will find your own, very personal path and be able to walk it with your partner. Partnerships will be supported and promoted by the new energy. Manipulation and abuse will be words of the past. They will no longer have any place on New Earth. Love and trust will be the glue of new relationships.

Do not shy away from transformation in yourself and in your relationships now. Flow with this new energy towards a new interaction. Cordiality and warmth of the heart will embrace you and strengthen your connections. Full hearts do not wound. Rather, they respect their neighbour, nature, and Earth. Be grateful to life!

These statements are to give you courage and confidence in this phase of transition, in order to enable you to welcome the new full of hope.

With Courage towards a Higher Vibrational Octave

Many people are currently living alone without a partner they love. They don't understand why they have to master their lives alone. Relationships break apart and cause deep wounds in those involved. Many children are brought up by a single parent, missing the other or never having met them at all. These conditions are highly painful for everyone involved. They cause upheaval that reaches to the core of one's being.

Every life experiences pervasive learning processes that eventually leads humans along their paths, dissolves old blocks and patterns, and initiate a new beginning. The upheaval that accompanies a human life is not all negative, but also an opportunity to attract new energies and to let go of old things.

This is comparable to the seasons. Spring always follows after winter. A dark night ends in sunrise. These rhythms are contained in everything, be it learning or growth processes.

The higher-vibrational energies now make more and more people aware of their living conditions and learning processes, enabling them to develop further on their paths. This is about development of their selves. They move from the chrysalis to become a butterfly who can fly freely in any direction and develop unhindered.

It is surely difficult while one is in the middle of such a learning process. However, I would like to show you the scope of such learning processes from a certain distance in order to give you the courage to boldly continue on your path, even if it may be stony here and there. Whatever you have transformed will never return. It will be dissolved!

However, do not be shocked to find patterns that you believe dissolved returning in some form – at times years after the fact. Various aspects of a block may reappear in order to be removed once more, and forever. A block will, therefore, be transformed level my level. That new, liberated energy will become the tool of your lives.

Cordial warmth flows into the liberated levels. Only love can heal injury and raise relationships onto a new level of understanding and forgiveness. Transformations are always connected to love. It is love for yourselves and for your neighbours. The abundance of this energy makes new beginnings integrated matters that enable you to set out for new shores, supported by the accelerated energy.

The next-higher octave of your consciousness cannot be climbed while weighed down by old ballast. It is now the nature of things that all humans are going through learning processes. The responsibility for solving those is with every individual. Your free will is going to determine your process of consciousness. The corresponding energies are at your disposal. You can choose freely! Trust in this energy. It will take you right to your goal. However, you must give yourself the time you need for it. Feel inside the process, and ask your higher selves – your divinity – to advise and lead you. If you are experiencing strong emotion, it is advisable to wait until you have developed a certain distance from the issue, so that you can tackle the next step from the depth of your being. Any targeted step, no matter how small, will bring you trust in yourselves and in your guidance. You are truly not alone. You do not have to get through this on your own. The spiritual world is aware of your problems and fears. It will gladly give you a helping hand. Of course, you will have to take the steps on your own. However, it is helpful to feel oneself be taken by the hand and led for part of the way.

The new, accelerated energy will make you aware of cosmic Love. This is the Love that keeps everything together in the micro- and macro-cosmos. That Love will dissolve your fears. Fears cannot stand next to that new Love. They will dissolve like mist in the sun. This accelerated energy will, therefore, help you more than ever to solve your problems. It will carry you through your learning processes. As I have mentioned, you will have to walk this path on your own. Your responsibility towards yourselves is with every individual. My words are to give you the courage to face your issues, to boldly attack them and to process them.

The growth steps every individual manages to take will benefit the greater whole: your families, your societies, your countries, and Earth. If you want to help the whole, if you desire peace on Earth, then start to work on yourselves. If you are in harmony with yourselves, you will radiate peace. That peace is needed now by everyone and by the whole. Peace can only be developed based on harmony. A peaceful, human society will then be ready to establish contact with its cosmic siblings.

Do not believe that this will take centuries to happen. No: the current energy of ascension into the Fifth Dimension will carry and guide you. You will manage things that you had barely dared dream of before. The residents of Earth will be raised up by this process. They can contribute to the cosmic dance and contribute as equal partners.

The War of Wars

Mankind has been fighting among itself for millennia. These conflicts are virtually always about power. The longest war of mankind, which is still ongoing, however, is the one between the genders. It, too, is about claims to power and domination. That conflict is now slowly nearing its end, to be replaced by partnership. The female and the male principles both have some very specific qualities that will now be connected in partnership to become integrated humanity. Everyone carries the female and male aspect in themselves, no matter their sex. That also means that the internal conflict between those forces will achieve a consensus, in order to manifest towards the outside. The current goal is that all individuals must now become integrated humans – a process that requires responsibility for themselves and for the others.

A man will never be able to bear children. He has other obligations. He will protect the woman during her pregnancy, support her creative attributes and help manifest them.

The female is the receiving and the male is the active principle. In order to be active, one first must receive! For example, ideas must be received – thought out – before they can be manifested. A great treasure of talents is unused in your societies, waiting to be accessed. Creative qualities need calm and quiet in order to be born so that they can be manifested on the outside. These are two different talents that will only lead to success together.

Large, Earth-changing achievements will manifest through the cooperation of sexes. These will be achievements that support mankind and Earth, and that will, thereby, create New Earth.

Competition between the sexes will dissolve. That energy is needed to rebirth new mankind and Earth. No one can delegate that transformation to others. Everyone is affected by this and must contribute to the process. Do not be surprised to see many men become softer and more receptive, and women become more assertive. Everyone will work on their talents in that area in order to harmonise them. That process has been topical in certain societies for a while. Now it will happen globally, and reach even highly patriarchal societies.

The new energy reaches all people and transforms old paradigms, no matter how your societies are built. The male and female principle is one divine creation – a UNITY.

Your holy scriptures have been inspired by God, but often written by men. Recognise the manipulations contained in them. No sex is inferior to the other. You are all divine, and God is not male or female.

The war between the sexes is nearing its end. It will be replaced by harmonisation of the female and male principles. There is still much to do, and many transformations to complete. The accelerated energy will let you harvest what you have sown. Peace will be able to unfold on Earth. This will truly be one of the greatest achievements of mankind. It will help you sustainably transform all your other issues. All doors will then be opened wide for your participation in the cosmic network. Your cosmic siblings are supporting this process. They are yearning for your arrival. Their joy will be great when they can finally embrace you and give you the place in the galactic family that you are due.

The Genetic Code

The genetic code that is visible to you is made up from two strands. In fact, however, you possess twelve such strands that are now being unravelled in order to allow the development of your multidimensional consciousness. What your scientists have been unable to decipher so far, and considered to be junk DNA, does have its purpose and use. The accelerated solar emanations that have been flowing onto Earth for a while will now enable this DNA to take over its original task again. Humans have the same DNA as their cosmic siblings. You are the cosmic seed after all, who volunteered to support Earth and mankind in their development. Do not be surprised to finally find talents in yourself that you never knew of. You will start to remember your cosmic roots, and you will suddenly realise that everything is connected – here on Earth and in the cosmos alike. The great illusion of separation is a Third- and Fourth-Dimensional quality that will dissolve as you ascend into the Fifth Dimension. Your scientists are beginning to discover the quality of the connection of everything to everything. Soon, everyone will be aware of this. It will help mankind solve its problems. The male and female principles will be connected on the inside and outside alike. The unfolding of your genetic code will support harmonisation of polarities. Though everyone must perform their own transformation work, you will be supported by the high, accelerated energy in your efforts. Clinging to old paradigms and codices will become more and more difficult. First, this will lead to radicalisation. Once the opposing forces have exhausted themselves, a merger will be possible. Trust in this evolutionary process. It is impossible to reverse anymore. The cosmic wave embraces Earth and her humans, and raises it onto a higher octave of being. Accordingly, old societal structures are no longer compatible with the new, high energy. They will collapse. New representatives of the people will try to transform human societies with progressive forces. These new societies that are founded on the respect of every individual will preserve their respective traditions, provided that they give every individual the freedom to develop. No difference will be made between man and woman anymore. Being human will take precedence. That is not a utopia. It is in your near future. Prepare for it, so that you will be able to ride on this new wave of evolution unhindered that will carry you to the paradise of Earth that you have created with your love and your awareness.

Love is the core of the message that I bring to you. This is love for ourselves, for others, for Earth, and for your cosmic siblings. Love will be the new essence of your connection with All-That-Is. Love is the energy that keeps the micro- and macrocosmos together and that connects everything to everything. We are all one in the ONE. It is our divine attribute, the purpose of our existence. This is the reason for these messages, the help of your cosmic siblings and the untiring effort of your fellow humans who have prepared this path for you. This ascent will only be possible in love as a whole. Only this will open the doors to paradise.

Your scientists will soon find that there is more than those two DNA strands alone. They will reach the depths of DNA and find substances they cannot quite explain yet. Trust in what you see and let go of old, linear paradigms. Try approaching this from a multidimensional perspective. Science will soon develop quantum leaps in many different specialisations. Linear thought will be expanded and pushed into quantum values. This will be an entirely new approach that will change the view of things. The influence of accelerated energies will carry you beyond the borders of your old manner of thinking and take you into multidimensional realms. A linear approach to setting tasks will also only permit you to see linear facts. Time is working for you. It will overturn the old thought patterns and let you increasingly develop an integrated view of things. Many things will become easy to comprehend for you. Those processes are now happening in every person. Of course, they particularly affect specialists who have made thinking, studying and research part of their everyday lives. In the next fifty years, incredible scientific innovations will be developed and benefit mankind, harmonisation of the polarities will allow achievements to serve the whole, rather than being abused only for the purpose of war. Certain innovations will only be possible once the consciousness of mankind will also use them for the good of Earth and man. Your manner of thinking and feeling will affect your every activity. Your reason and your hearts will give your cohabitation and your activities a basic direction. Mankind and Earth will be at the focus of your solution approaches.

Greed, envy, and fury are part of the old paradigms. They will no longer have any place on New Earth. Thanks to the loss of old, negative braking forces, you will develop at exponentially increasing speed.

Illnesses and physical aging will no longer strain your communities, since your integrated view of things will enable you to take preventative and healing action. Since everyone is fully responsible for themselves, they will do anything to be able to live healthily and actively and to contribute to society.

This will give humans fulfilled lives. Being human is the motto. Society, economy, religions, and nations will be permeated by this law. It will become the most natural thing in the world. As you will notice, I am speaking of humans, rather than women and men. That is nothing but pigeonholing! Being human is something that every individual must develop for themselves. Feel inside yourselves and open your hearts to yourselves and the whole. This will bring about incredibly positive, pervasive change and turn Earth into your paradise.

Abundance

Earth, with whom you are sharing your lives, is incredibly rich in every respect. You can enjoy the most beautiful, diverse landscapes, and many different climates. You have developed different regional traditions and rituals. Your flora and fauna is as diverse as humans are. An increasable plethora of living beings are now ascending into the Fifth Dimension together with Mother Earth. If you consider that the rising energies now permeate everything, you can imagine that great changes are ahead in yourselves, in nature, and in Earth. You have been exposed to these accelerated energies for a long time. This is reflected in the collapse of your old paradigms already, both societal, religious, and economic in nature. Those old paradigms must give way to new structures now. This is a process that takes time. You will work creatively for new solutions around the world, and find that your problems cannot be solved nationally. You will need to find global approaches. You are one mankind here on this planet. You are now learning how carefully you must treat Earth. She is your home and your hearth. Climate disasters have shown you that you are responsible for the whole. Egoistical territorial decisions are no longer acceptable. You will develop international, and even intercontinental solution approaches, not only referring to climate and exploitation of Earth, but also to unite the many different populations into one human family. Just like in every family, you will learn to respect your differences, support each other's talents, and compensate for each other's weaknesses. Planet Earth, Gaia, or Terra, is your shared basis and your home. That association, that symbiosis, will become increasingly clear in the human minds.

Women also have a more direct access to Earth through their cycles of birth and menstruation. They will be of invaluable help to mankind. Yes, they will be the midwives of the rebirth of Earth into a higher octave of existence. Liberate your women, to enable them to exercise their entire potential. You men will support their ideas and put them into practice. This arrangement will benefit everything, from very private to global scopes. Your future generations will have your developed talents and abilities to look over the rims of your teacups encoded in their genes and develop them further in turn. The symbiotic relationship between Earth and her humans will bring the long-desired abundance to everything - the Golden Age of Earth and mankind.

It isn't like a land of plenty where everything is given to you without any effort on your part. No, you must put in effort and contribute to your lives and your heritage – though of course the accelerated solar emanations will support you. Mankind turning towards an integrated life and contributing respect and love to its activities will truly achieve quantum leaps. The accelerated energy has already sensitised great parts of mankind. Your goal is coming closer and closer. Trust in this snowball principle. Developments will become exponential and your dreams will come true.

The plethora in all of its facets will enrich your lives on Earth and you will enjoy them, pass them on and let them flow.

The pending changes will make cooperation and everyday life on Earth easier and more harmonious. Let go of all that is old and focus on creative solutions for your issues. You may find that you need to change tricky structures that have accompanied you for centuries and that have become part of your traditions. Believe me: certain traditions are incredibly inhibitive for your future development now. They no longer match the new humans you are now turning into. Painful processes are about to occur. They will give you greater freedom and will support the community on Earth. Old paradigms may be destroyed with brutal force or change step by step in a process-oriented manner. You can decide how to handle the innovations. You are responsible here on Earth. No one can take that burden away from you. The simplest way is surely changing yourself and letting that new energy become part of your environment. Everyone is affected by this. The more people face the changes, the more quickly and effectively new structures will be born. If you keep your male and female sides in balance in yourself, for example, you will contribute this to your family and to your environment. Old structures will automatically have to be rethought and new ones must be developed. That process will liberate you all and let you participate in the abundance of Earth. Earth belongs to all people, no matter where they live and where they are at home.

The residents of Earth will not be homogeneous. Their diversity is part of their wealth, just as this is the case in the galactic civilisations. The energy of the heart connects everything and everyone. It bridges differences and leads to joint solutions. Open your hearts to your own matters, and then let that energy flow into your environment. The resonance of your environment will surprise you! The energy of the heart will bring you that interhuman abundance. It will promote cooperation. Opposition will have served its purpose. Wars and armed destruction will soon be things of your past. You will approach each other with warmth and compassion, and welcome the plethora of your differences. This new, golden age will flow into all facets of human contacts and enrich them. Cohesion among the residents of Earth will be developed through the heart. Only that quality of the heart will guarantee a peaceful future for you. Love is a human right. It is an inalienable asset. It is the essence of all life, no matter if here on Earth or in the cosmos. Claim that essential right for yourselves now. It's your basic nutrition. Without love, you are only surviving! I have emphasised "for yourselves". That is the most essential thing. Do not look for love on the outside, but inside you. Discover and spread the wealth inside you, and let it make you invulnerable and independent.

Lovers choosing each other under these prerequisites will give each other the freedom and support they need for a true partnership. The new romantic relationships will no longer serve as a replacement for one's own vacuum of love.

As you can see, the current changes are not only happening on the outside, but also affect your deep, personal levels. Like matter is permeated entirely by the new energy, so will your minds. You are facing a radical change on the inside and outside. You are facing the rebirth of Earth into a higher octave of existence and development of humanity into the higher race of Adam Kadmon.

Can you now understand the great blessing that it is to live on Earth now, to experience and help design this rebirth?

Liberation

The new developments that I have explained will trigger a process of liberation in your minds, but also in your everyday lives, and in handling of your daily tasks. That will have a global effect. Implementation of many structural reconciliations and innovations will take a lot less time and work that it used to in the past. Integrated liberation for everyone is about to commence now, carrying you to a higher human level of existence. You will be surprised to find that you can suddenly find a consensus for old, tedious issues. For example, solutions that can be accepted by everyone will be found for strongly polar opinions and plans. Energy is now strongly accelerated, which will help you dissolve old, structural encrustations and to work creatively to develop new modes of life. That energy will now harmonise the tension between the polarities step by step. Rivalling parties will increasingly be able to come together and develop solutions that work for all parties. These are no wonders that are happening now. It reflects the development of mankind into a higher level of existence. Of course, everyone now needs to integrate that new energy into their bodies and minds. They may find themselves facing issues in adjustment, such as pain that they cannot place or outbursts of emotions that you are unfamiliar with. In such cases, it is advisable to find stillness and centre yourselves. Trust in this process and feel inside you. Support your bodies with rest, appropriate food, and exercise. Everyone knows instinctively what is good for them. Listen to your bodies' signals and give them what they need. Your bodies must prepare for the dimensional change and gradually integrate the higher energy. Its entire atomic structure has been vibrating more quickly for a while now. That process is now further accelerating in this time of transition into the Fifth Dimension. Your bodies will excrete all of your old burdens that you are now transforming as slags. Support them with the corresponding therapies.

Your bodies are your manifestation opportunities here on Earth. Treat them with respect and support. They are part of the unit you call SELF, made up of body, mind, and soul. Your souls are located in the multidimensional space. Your minds and bodies now move into a higher dimension. This is a process that happens slowly and is connected to your state of consciousness. Never before has it been able to complete such a dimensional change with a living body on Earth. That is why it is so important to observe the framework conditions and to consciously contribute to this process. That means integrating new energy continually and stabilising oneself and one's body in the new reality. I would like to point you to Mother Earth to help you stabilise yourself. She, too, must continually integrate new energy. Contact her! Spend plenty of time in nature! Ground yourselves! She will be a great support for you and teach you to ride this wave of energy physically and mentally alike. The wave will guide you where you need to go. Your real task is merely in stabilising yourself in the Here-and-Now. That will automatically flush you into the Fifth Dimension.

For a great many people, this challenge will bring about a new state of consciousness. Many people will want to remain in their old energy as well. They will close themselves to the innovations and cling to the status quo. Breaking out of one's prison and proceeding into the new and unknown is surely not simple and takes courage and trust. In the current high energy emission, "stalling" in the old is similar to "swimming against the current" and, as a result, will be very exhausting and tiring. And, in some cases, it can be fatal.

I urgently advise you to enjoy this unique goal here on Earth and to free yourselves from your prison. The new path ahead of you will return you more and more to yourselves. You will once again become what you have truly always been. You are approaching great times now.

They are times of fulfilment in all respects. It is what you call paradise or the Garden of Eden!

A Supreme Millennium

You entered the new millennium a few years ago. Changes are now a matter of course. You have already gotten used to it to a degree. The speed at which events unfold demands great flexibility and stability from you in everyday life. You will have to learn to live in the Here-and-Now more and more. The past is apart from you, and the future is more and more difficult to foresee. Life in the Here-and-Now is the quintessence of life. It will bring you stability and make fears dissolve. Great, sustainable deeds can be born from that calm. These will be deeds that are fresh and not prejudiced by old guidelines that belong to the past. In this condition, you will be able to access the universal source directly. Your intuition will connect you to spheres that are otherwise closed to you. Since everything is interconnected, you can find unusual solutions for your issues, and develop new concepts. An entirely new manner of thought will unfold. This will involve receiving inspiration from other spheres. Your scientists will use that new help, and develop great innovations that will be of immense use for mankind. The great inventions have already been perceived intuitively on Old Earth. This will be entirely normal on New Earth. That help and gift will, of course, not be limited to scientists alone, but apply to everyone who is active creatively, both in art and in everyday life.

As the energy vibrations gain in strength, they will dissolve the veil that separates you from other dimensions. This expands your point of view with every day. You will perceive a higher or broader perspective of things. You will feel embedded in the universe and gain access to All-That-Is. Unimaginable wealth in all segments will become accessible to you. Universal knowledge will be distributed on Earth, heal mankind, and help it comprehend itself as a cosmic being. Resurrection of mankind, its return to its cosmic siblings, and maturation of the cosmic seed is just ahead here on Earth!

You will all be able to fully enjoy the harvest of your millennia of efforts and contribute to the whole as multidimensional beings.

Contact with your cosmic siblings will strongly influence your life on Earth. They will teach you new techniques, e.g. in promotion of interaction, in communication, in the transport industry, or in healing. Great breakthroughs will happen in that segment, in particular in prevention. Humans will learn to keep their bodies young and healthy for their own joy and to relieve society. Degenerative diseases will disappear, and genetic ones will be healed. Everyone will take full responsibility for themselves, both physically and mentally, and contribute to their societies and to the whole.

The development of mankind since the commencement of the first millennium has been extraordinary. This new millennium, however, will bring you unimaginable developments. These developments and innovations not only refer to technology and quality of life. Mankind itself will experience the greatest changes inside itself. The quality of the heart will be the motivation in all areas of life. Harmonisation of emotions will follow. Envy, hate, fury, aggression, etc. will dissolve and be unable to stand up in light of the new energy.

You were surprised about the interhuman progress when you entered the Fifth Dimension in December 2012 already. It will continue to develop exponentially and lead you into the Golden Age.

Humans and Earth will be at the centre of the new era. Humane, fulfilled lives will be available to everyone. Wealth will be accessible to everyone. The hardships of Old Earth will be dissolved. The polarity of rich/poor, educated/uneducated, etc. will be harmonised. This will release enormous positive energies in each of you, enabling you to design your lives freely. Pressure and stress will become foreign words from a time long past.

Mankind that is able to unfold freely and that acts from its heart chakra will do all it can to connect to each other and to engage in exchange. This multicultural society is a great treasure of Earth. It is a great reservoir of deeds and creative implementation. Every culture will contribute to the good of mankind and of Earth. Humans will see themselves as a global family on Earth, and be willing to go beyond the borders of their planet and to venture into space. Contact with their cosmic siblings of Light will let them access their place in space, and enable them to participate in the galactic councils, and to present their matters there.

Humans must, therefore, develop into a higher octave of existence first in order to pass through the galactic gates.

Invasion, exploitation, occupation, war-like projects – all of those will be foreign words. Though this may still seem incredible, you will soon cease to understand those words and deeds. Mankind is undergoing a great evolutionary leap, supported by the cosmic vibration. Loving hearts will not fight, battle, or kill. Loving hearts will take responsibility for their deeds and support each other. I know that all of this sounds very unlikely, and like a fairy-tale. Trust me: you are now on this path into your future, which is not that far away.

The flora and fauna of Earth will support humans. You will find that your new emission will nurture all of your environment. You will work the land together with the Earth spirits, fairies, and gnomes, who will support you. By understanding your symbiotic association with Earth, you will be able to cooperate with her to fix deficits in certain regions. For example, you can energise fields or call in rain. The genes of your indigenous peoples know those rituals. They are intimately familiar with the entity of Mother Earth. They will help you! You are developing into Light and making use of your roots, in order to contribute your share to the whole in an integrated manner. All talents that you have acquired and applied in your many incarnations are now available to you. Do not be surprised if you suddenly remember them. Your DNA contains your very personal history with Earth and with the cosmos. That treasure trove will be available to you. The highly accelerated energy will now do its share and advance you step by step towards your great potential. Do not forget that you are now developing into multidimensional beings. The limitations and impairments of the Third and Fourth Dimensions will very soon be overcome, and you will be reborn into the Fifth Dimension.

This is a dimension that you on Earth are not familiar with and that you need to integrate into your bodies and your everyday lives first. This dimension will be quite different from what you have known so far. Be happy to continue on your path into Light. Your hardships will soon be over. The gate to the Fifth Dimension is open in order to receive you. Mother Earth and her humans experience a blissful ascension into a higher octave of existence.

Claims to Power

Egotistical claims to power are your, and everyone's, greatest enemy. That scenario is moving towards its downfall, in political, social, economic, and religious respects. This will lead to enormous upheavals that will hit every individual severely. Man now needs to learn to be responsible. They are the authorities in their own lives. They will no longer find any help from the outside. They will engage in exchange with the outside, but will find their purpose in themselves, on the inside. This will start out in a careful approach and some chaotic conditions. In the end, however, every individual will grow strong in themselves and contribute to their co-creatorship.

Processes of great, pervasive changes are ahead of you. They will take a while to happen. Continue patiently on your path into the Light and trust in your very personal process. It will open up your multidimensional potential and turn you into what you have always been: cosmic co-creators.

Looking back later, you will hardly be able to believe your own immaturity and helplessness just a few years ago. This – new – self-worth that you are experiencing will release enormous energies inside you. You will be able to use them for yourselves, your society and Earth. The deep recognition of yourselves will lead you to your personal talents and your potential, which will trigger a great creative exchange for everyone's good. You will hardly be able to imagine the talents concealed inside you and only waiting to be finally liberated. You have all registered innumerable incarnations here on Earth or in the cosmos in your DNA. They were incarnations in which you have acquired and exercised a variety of talents. That potential will now unfold step by step in the next years, to be available to you and to Earth. This truly is great wealth that your societies are accessing now. Boldly work to free and use your talents. Open your limitations and start looking at yourselves from a multidimensional perspective. Leave your narrow mental pigeonholes and admit vast and unlimited opportunities.

This process will not be limited to some few people. It is a global project. The expansion of your humanity will happen exponentially. Everyone's wealth will be exchanged, and everyone will be able to participate in the treasures of every individual. Do not forget that we are all connected to each other in the ONE. Our co-creatorship will serve to honour our source.

As multidimensional beings, we are all connected to each other – in the cosmos and on Earth. We all work with our treasures in order to bring the Light of the ONE to perfection. The heavenly seraphim have taken over Earth and will continue on with it into eternity!

Claims to Possession

You are all aware that you cannot take your material assets along when you move on after death! They are merely a learning process in your lives. They enable you to complete your work and projects. They give you a certain freedom to design your lives, to develop and support projects, and to enjoy material wealth. Let this richness flow, to allow it to develop further and benefit others as well. Greedy accumulation and hoarding matches an approach to safety that you will soon be able to shed. You are only as safe as mankind as a whole is. Once the wealth of Earth is accessible to everyone, once the polarity in your economic world harmonises, then the terms of greed, stockpiling, hoarding, envy, and jealousy will lose their basis and disappear from your vocabulary. The material wealth achieved will be available to everyone and support everyone.

The collapse of your old economic paradigms already proves that they are not compatible with the new high vibration. New structures are now being built step by step and adjust to new humans and new Earth. Great fundamental changes are ahead that will affect all of mankind. Your emotional and rational wealth of knowledge is integrated into the new paradigms and will take on integrated forms. The quality of the heart will enter into this area as well! A new economy is designed for humans and for Earth, rather than against it. The general whole will be considered, rather than just a very few. You will have to be highly creative in this respect in the next few years. After all, the rising high vibrations will only permit compatible structures. Be ready to adjust the new structures to the new energy many times if they are to survive. Money equals energy. Let it flow!

Possessiveness as you know it today will give way to new principles. You will be carried by this globally developed wealth. This will give you the safety that you need and inspire you to contribute as well.

Your current possessions do, at times, go far beyond what you need for a safe, comfortable life. Possession can possess as well. That means that it will make you unfree, idle, and immobile. The new energy will no longer allow you to cling to material assets. Since everything will continually increase its vibrations, leading to spiritualisation of matter, the conditions of possession will loosen up. Everything is connected to everything else. What "belongs" to whom then? Unlimited exchange will happen! Mine-yours will be harmonised. This is still difficult to imagine for you now. It will not happen instantaneously, but it is a process of your consciousness that will coincide with the increase of vibrations. You will, in a manner of speaking, grow into this new quality. There will be no disowning and battles. Claims to "possession" will become permeable. As mentioned, this will be a harmonious growth process that keeps up with the increase of energy. The more spiritualised matter is, the fewer limits will it have. These are Fifth-Dimensional aspects that you will slowly grow into. As you continue into the Fifth Dimension, many old conditions and aspects will be dissolved. An utterly new era is maturing. That is why we consider it a rebirth of Earth in a new cycle. Do not forget that mankind also develops in this direction. It is like the opening of a gate that has long hindered you from free movement. You are now assessing this development from a Third- or Fourth-Dimensional perspective. Believe me: paradigms will change fundamentally in the Fifth Dimension. This will go far beyond mere adjustments. It is, in a figure of speech, like finding yourself unable to fit into the shoes you wore as children. You have outgrown them! This is the manner in which you will let go of many conditions in order to fully enjoy the new octave.

Earth will become paradise as heavens and Earth merge! You have surely heard that about the Fifth Dimension before. Well, can you imagine that it would have fences and bars? Hardly, I would think. I can see you smile.

Tomorrow and the Day after Tomorrow

The energy flooding Earth from your sun will increase steeply and influence your everyday lives. You are about to enter a time of great changes. Old structures are breaking apart and new ones must be created. Since energy increases again and again, repeated adjustments to new structures must be made during that time. A decision may soon cease to be acceptable, and new opportunities may need to be considered. You are living in a time of unrest. You must revise your life plan time and time again, accept new situations and let go of the old. This will be incredible training for your flexibility. You will no longer be able to return to your old structures. That will be very hard for you mentally. This is why it is so important that you are aware of why all of this is happening. It will help you surf on this energy wave and develop trust in this process.

Earth is changing the dimension in which it is at home. It is moving more closely to the central sun, thereby receiving a lot more Light from its own sun. This is a cosmic process. The entire solar system is affected by this.

You will be embedded more closely in the galactic area in future. Energetic interaction with your neighbourhood will become perceptible to you. The entire galactic sector is increasing in energy.

Your bodies must integrate this accelerated energy in every single atom. You are now able to manage this dimensional change with your bodies. That surely will not be easy. You will be challenged by it. It will demand a price from you. Therefore, question your discomfort, your sudden pain, your illnesses. What are your bodies trying to tell you? Do they simply need rest in order to manage energetic integration, or do they need to be healed of patterns that are no longer viable? It is advisable to focus intensely on your physical aspects now so that you can complete this dimensional change with your bodies. Your bodies are giving you a unique opportunity of experiencing biological mutations of a greater scope while alive, and to help design them. You will truly practice what co-creatorship means now. You are what you think and feel! It is a great responsibility, but also a unique opportunity. Your bodies are ever-changing. Take control and create the bodies you wish to have, and that will support you. Only you can make decisions on your own bodies. You are obligated only towards yourselves. You are your own fate!

The increase of energy will continue persistently, until Earth has reached the energy level she needs to complete the dimensional change. All humans will have to handle that energy, but every individual will decide whether they want to complete the dimensional change. This ascension into the Fifth Dimension will be initiated by the conscious people themselves. No one can perform this transition for another, or take someone else along with them. This makes it all the more important to be aware of your own needs. You can only live and change through yourselves.

After ascending into the Fifth Dimension, the energy is further accelerated, though no longer as strongly as it was in the transition phase. You will need the time to get used to that high energy, and to integrate it. New paradigms will be created in all areas of life. New technologies will be discovered, and societies will be restructured. You have, in a way, arrived at a new level. As is common after birth, you are facing great learning phases. More highly vibrating, spiritualised matter is subject to different laws. You will also transition from a linear into a non-linear age. Everything will be more strongly present in the Here-and-Now. You will be fully conscious of that when the time has come. The new laws will allow you to drive great scientific discoveries and innovations. Your world view will be revolutionised and answer questions that you have long been dealing with.

Harmonisation of the polarities will liberate great energy reserves in every individual, enabling them to become fully responsible for themselves.

The Fifth-Dimensional energy will continue to increase, bringing you this "Golden Age" that was foretold in your scriptures. This is a process that the next generations will be allowed to share.

The Third- and Fourth-Dimensional aspects of separation will be overcome. You will recognise that everything is connected to everything else, and that we are all one in the ONE. The cosmos and Earth will become one. The resulting exchange with your cosmic siblings will become a matter of course. Space flight, dematerialisation, and materialisation – which you call "beaming" – can be learned and used.

Showing you the new developments is difficult, since you will understand them from a Third- and Fourth-Dimensional perspective. You are also lacking the necessary vocabulary right now.

For the moment, limit yourselves to short-term perspectives and trust in this unique process of ascension into the paradise Earth, and into a new, phenomenal cycle of Earth.

The Bright Side of Life

You are facing great transformations right now, both in your private lives and globally. Nevertheless, do not forget to live your lives fully and to enjoy them to the utmost. Your sensuality will show you the bright side of life, be it in the form of a beautiful sunrise, a rainbow, little daily attentions, a smile, a tender touch, etc. This is not a dreary time, but quite the opposite. You will be brought back to yourselves, and to what you are feeling at any given moment: the Here-and-Now. Do not let chaotic conditions disconcert you. Look at little everyday things that surround and support you, and be grateful for this eventful time that you are experiencing now on Earth. It is exciting to move into new areas and to burst through your limitations.

New companions will walk by your side for a part of your paths. Mutual exchange will fertilise you and help you find your own way, to develop and implement your potential. Humans are social beings. Nevertheless, it is important that every individual go into stillness and solitude now and then in order to return strengthened in their centre to engage in mutual exchange once more. That exchange will become more loving and based on compassion now, the more intensely the new energy permeates Earth. Mutual help and support will increase. You will become increasingly aware that you are all connected to each other. All of mankind is already able to manage this ascension. Some are already aware of this process. They can take the others by the hand for a while. However, they can also simply let their Lights shine. That Light will brighten up the darkness and bring clarity into your surroundings.

Polarities will gradually harmonise now. Consensus will be found more and more where there are difficulties. Finding that consensus is a process that expresses the consciousness for everyone involved. Even though a problem may seem impossible to solve at first, the increasing energy reduces polarity peaks and makes a solution visible on a higher level. Imagine this like a triangle, with the two polarity corners at the bottom and the solution or consensus in the middle at the top. The problem at hand will always be raised up. In other words: you need to look at every problem from a higher position in order to develop possible solutions. The liberation from your limitations will now be strongly promoted by the rising energy, enabling you to solve issues that keep you busy. Trust in this process, and recognise your growth, and the change of your consciousness, with entirely new solution models. For example, you will create social achievements that you could barely dream of in the past.

The bright side of life means that the darkness is enlightened, and that clarity is increased, and laws are made visible, as a result. Since more energy is being flushed onto Earth now, more Light will reach the atomic matter. Matter is spiritualised, which means that it will change from a Third- and Fourth-Dimensional density to a Fifth-Dimensional one. The atomic structure will oscillate more quickly, enabling better access for Light. All matter is, in fact, Light in a condensed, differentiated condition. In fact, everything is energy that is now given a higher vibration. If your bodies contain more Light, your mental status and behaviours will necessarily change as well. This in turn will affect your societies and the environment. In other words: harmonisation of the polarities is caused by increased Light energy, since the polarities will balance themselves out anew. Newly created structures in all areas of life will be caused by great emissions of the current Light energy. The seed of innovation is part of that energy. You merely need to learn handling that high energy personally and globally, integrating it and working with it. Great challenges are ahead for you to fully integrate it. You must let go of the old and obsolete.

The increase of Light energy has been ongoing for years. It is now increasing drastically with the ascension into the Fifth Dimension. You are now forced to deal with yourselves. Your negative patterns are now presented to you in order to be transformed. A gigantic process of healing is happening on all levels now. Negative aspects are gradually being transformed and dissolved. Your DNA is being aligned with a Fifth-Dimensional quality, raising you up to become the higher race of Adam Kadmon and enabling you to engage in an exchange as partners with your cosmic siblings. This process will let you understand and align interaction on Earth anew, and to continue your journey with Earth.

I hope that this great perspective is giving you courage when you are temporarily stuck in an issue and unable to understand the world around you. Stop for a moment to give this great energy the opportunity to integrate. New things will develop, and your problems will be solved. Of course, you must contribute to New Earth as well. The accelerated energy is your help. It will show you an integrated approach.

Since everyone is now taking responsibility for their own lives, and surfing on the high energy, they will live on the bright side of life and contribute to the whole in fulfilment.

The Evolution of New Technologies

The increased vibrations will now gradually allow you to access the potential that has lain dormant in you for eons. You used to be at home on many different stars, with many different dimensional levels, and you have developed many learning processes everywhere, both on the level of the soul and of matter. Do not be surprised to suddenly find yourself overcome by incomprehensible thoughts and inspiration. The chambers in which your talents have been slumbering are about to open. Take the new ideas seriously and try to integrate them into your lives. You may also be contacted by spiritual helpers or cosmic siblings, since you have the equipment you need to implement their messages. I have already mentioned several times that we are all connected to each other. Once the necessary new energy is integrated, such contact can be established. Think about whether you want to accept and implement such messages. You are responsible here on Earth. In any case, see it as help from your spiritual and cosmic allies. Your spiritual and cosmic friends will always introduce themselves to you and ask whether you wish to receive a message. You will clearly recognise that this does not stem from your subconscious. The energy will differ from your own.

Those messages, as well as your own ideas, will bring incredible innovation to mankind in the near future. They will help you design New Earth. They will be technical, economical, as well as societal innovations. You are about to reinvent your lives on Earth. That needs all the treasures available to you: your own and the cosmic ones.

Breakthroughs in physics and mechanics, medicine, and biology, will follow in quick succession, and affect everyone's everyday lives. That progress will show you a new image of Earth and her place in the cosmos, but also supplement your philosophies and make them visible. You will recognise a higher perspective of things, and live according to it. Economy will take place as a helper of mankind.

The new technologies will support humans. This is why they will be developed and applied only once human consciousness has achieved its ascension and reached the required vibrational level. Certain technologies can only be used by conscious and responsible humans!

Areas such as transport are revolutionised. You will be working with free energy, similar to the way your cosmic siblings are using space flight. This will bring mankind more closely together. The distances that separated them will be faster to overcome.

Technologies that you may still consider utopian now will help and support mankind in developing the new societies here on Earth. Management of everyday life will be easier for everyone in the Fifth Dimension, enabling people to focus more on being human. This is the motto of the new era. Compassion for everything alive will take priority.

If consciousness determines life, material assets will no longer benefit just some few. Global balance will occur. The wealth of Earth belongs to everyone. Harmonisation of the polarities will flow into this area as well, eradicating hunger and suffering on Earth. Earth conceals sufficient treasures to let everyone live in safety and prosperity. Just distribution of the assets is, therefore, mandatory.

The new technologies will make this distribution easier and allow you to reach any location on Earth. This exchange will have wonderful consequences and strongly promote the community among the people of Earth.

Today's crisis regions experience a special participation of the Earth's population, and this support will give those people the strength and courage to build new structures for life. All of mankind is only as strong as its minorities are. This awareness will be the motivation for the new societies – harmonisation of mankind will be the result.

Since the polarities are gradually growing less severe now, mankind will be given the opportunity to develop further in Light and to contribute to the whole as a cosmic partner. Harmonisation of the polarities will be an incredible liberation for every individual. They can then use the newly released energy for their development, and for development of mankind.

Higher-vibrational matter will change laws of nature. Handling of material things will have to be learned anew. This handling will be easier, however, and mankind will be better supported. In many areas, energies will be released to support you and give you more freedom that you can use for yourselves. Agitation and stress are no longer part of that world view. They will be replaced by relaxation and plenty.

The new technologies are not easy to explain. Some of them are not based on anything you know. Quantum leaps will be completed, since you are now dealing with a higher-vibrational matter that follows different laws. Those innovations will manifest step by step, always in resonance with the current vibration. That means that you will grow into entirely new dimensions and that you can recognise what is useful for you. Your changed, conscious awareness of things will let you develop new creations that will benefit humans and Earth.

Your education – your equipment - will not always help you. You need to learn to understand entirely new concepts. First, you will have to distance yourselves from what you have learned, in order to enable you to perform that quantum leap. You will have to newly approach, feel, and view things in an integrated manner. Your reason, as well as your feelings and sensuality, are needed now. Mankind will move into this new territory as a whole and explore it. I wish you great joy and success in this adventure.

The Flow of Energy

Your scientists have already perceived that your sun's energy and emanations on Earth are changing and increasing. Solar radiation has always been subject to cycles. Now, however, it is changing for a reason that is not yet understood.

Earth is embedded in a greater whole, in her own solar system in the Milky Way, your galaxy, and in our universe. The centre of your galaxy is now sending out high-quality radiation that the suns are absorbing and passing on to their planets. That radiation is Love, Light and information. It brightens up the darkest regions, makes them mature and turns them into zones with higher energetic oscillations. Earth and her solar system are now undergoing an increase of their vibrations, and a dimensional change. The higher the vibrations of a celestial body, the more spiritualised is its matter. The material density of Earth is changing. It is adjusting to the new dimension that will oscillate a lot more highly than the density of Old Earth. That new, high-quality energy must be absorbed in every single atom of Earth.

Earth is undergoing metamorphosis, from which it will be reborn in the new dimension or energy density after great changes.

This makes it logical that this process will bring about great changes on the inside and outside of Earth. Earth is freeing herself from old pressure and ballast in order to be able to absorb the high energy.

You humans – residents of Earth – are spirit in matter. That means that you are now experiencing this metamorphosis in order to be reborn into the new dimension. This rebirth will happen inside yourselves with many changes. You must also get rid of pressure and ballast, in order to fully integrate the new energy and in order to allow your bodies to accept this metamorphosis.

When I speak of your bodies, I also mean your minds, which are intricately connected to the material aspects. To allow integration of this high energy, I advise, as mentioned, that you seek stillness periodically, to take downtimes in order to continue once again centred in yourselves. The information that you find in yourselves will help you be in the right place at the right time, and do the right things. Trust in your inner voice and your feelings will strengthen and help you be solid as a rock in this time of transition. Contact with Mother Earth, with whom you are living in symbiosis, gives you the strength and perseverance that you now need.

The flow of energy is comparable to your brooks and rivers. Even great amounts of water will not do any harm while they can flow and are not dammed in. Try to do the same with your bodies. Remove old ballast in the form of old behavioural patterns. Transform them, so that energy can flow unhindered, and particles of Light can reach all the way into your atomic structure. This will make your bodies more Light-filled and permeable, and heal them from their old, negative experiences. The more Light your body takes in, the more will you be able to model it to your needs. That will make you more and more into co-creators in your world. Your bodies are your opportunity for manifestation. You can influence its health and rejuvenation with your own information. The power of your thoughts will increase, enabling you to influence your lives as well as your environment. Be aware of your responsibility, and act under consideration and for the good of the whole.

Earth and her humans are about to venture into a higher level of existence, in order to better serve the ONE in community with their cosmic siblings, and to advance evolution. Earth and her humans will once again become consciously part of the cosmic family. They have always held that place, but were internally separated from it.

That separation is now nearing its end. This is like the return of the lost son or the lost daughter into the family circle, as your scriptures tell. You will be welcomed with great joy and compassion. Everyone has been yearning for your arrival. Understand the help of your cosmic siblings in this context. It is proof of their love for you.

Excesses

At the moment, you are still experiencing radicalisation of your polarities. For example, think of the male and female polarity in patriarchal societies, of the greedy economic system, the militant manipulations of some religions, etc. Those circumstances are hard to bear for those affected. It creates fear and insecurity. These are truly severe tests for mankind. Maintaining personal stability during this time is hard for everyone affected. My sympathy goes out to you. However, be assured that it will not take long before the energy level has reached the amplitude that will loosen up your living conditions and that will gradually make way for harmonisation of the polarities. It is like the passage through the eye of a needle: enormous contraction, a great release of old conditions, followed by a great liberation and re-orientation.

The tests mankind as a whole are undergoing will lead you to mastery and turn you into the ascended race of Adam Kadmon. It will make you multidimensional beings.

The love of your cosmic siblings is with you. They will support you as far as you permit it. They can see the upheaval you are going through precisely, and pay you great respect.

Target the new, Fifth--Dimensional conditions on Earth with the power of your thoughts. Create your world of peace – your paradise. Try to integrate as much Light in your bodies as you can. Design your environment for the good of Light and Love. Be steadfast! Soon, you will be able to reap the seed of your long incarnations on Earth. This was a long, and in parts difficult path that is now reaching its peak. You are on the final stretch before the finish line, once again required to draw on all your strength and motivation. You will soon be honoured as the victors. Your mission on Earth is almost over. The energy level of Earth is already so high that reversal is impossible. You have nearly reached your goal, and will be able to face the dimensional change calmly. The negative excesses of the polarities show you that the tension is increasing, until a consensus is striven for on a higher level. The originators of that tension will come together and develop new solutions. All humans are involved in this process, after all. Suppression and manipulation will no longer be possible.

Working and learning processes are now ahead of you on your further paths. It is creation of a new, human society here on Earth: a society that is enriched by many traditions and a society that understands itself as residents of Earth and that is connected to each other with the quality of the heart.

Confusion resulting from the current restructuring causes stress and instability. This will stop being part of your lives soon. As soon as the Fifth-Dimensional energy level is reached, they will dissolve, since the new structures can then apply, and adjustments are no longer appearing at the current cadence. You are going through a time of transition here on Earth. The old no longer applies and the new has not yet taken the place it is due. In these times, you will need great perseverance and trust in your personal process of evolution, and the one of Earth. Look ahead and do not mourn for the past. It is forever obsolete. The current learning processed in your private and social lives will take you to your core, and the purpose of your lives and of mankind. Believe me that this learning process will bring you great fulfilment and show you the wonderful whole in which you are embedded. Your participation in the universal happenings will show you qualities of space that will free all of mankind from their previous fates.

Welcome the new morning, and be grateful that you are allowed to contribute to this great rebirth of Earth and of mankind. Your souls will register this ascension quality and store it in their potential forever. You will become masters of ascension and of dimensional change. This is, truly, a wonderful competence.

Simultaneity

Your thoughts connect you to other people at the same time, no matter the distance. Over time, your telepathic skills will develop, and you will be able to receive clear messages from your fellow humans. That ability is already part of you, but has been used rarely so far and therefore has atrophied. The increase of energy will bring this skill increasingly to your awareness. Of course, it will take practice to develop this inborn talent and to use it every day, much in the same manner as you are using your mobile phones to write text messages. Unfolding that talent will be particularly useful for you. It is quite possible that the enormous solar radiation will deactivate your communication systems for shorter or longer periods of time.

I have already pointed out your responsibility towards your thoughts. Thoughts are forms of energy that will materialise and influence your present and your future alike. Choose the quality of your lives!

As you are used to from the telephone and internet, you will be connected to one or several of your fellow humans at the same time. You will call them and send them your message. It is quite similar in the telepathic area. Focus your thoughts on a person and pass on the desired message. With some exercise, the person you targeted will respond and in turn send a message. Try it out! You will find that it is becoming much simpler now, with the increased energy. Some other talents are also slumbering inside you. They will appear in the near future. Those talents will support and enrich your lives here on Earth.

The Here-and-Now is the scale to measure things by. It is the time that you truly spend on Earth and during which you can tap and use your potential.

The past and future is processed in the Here-and-Now, and the quality of the present sows the seeds for innovation. The present perspective will guide you in your future direction. You are the architects of your lives. You will determine your own path. The highest law here on Earth is that of free will. That requires you to be responsible for yourselves and for the whole.

In the Here-and-Now, you are experiencing fulfilment in symbiosis with Earth. Joy can only be experienced in this condition. The search for joy will bring you closer and closer to that status of being. The small and large events of the present will fill your hearts and your existence.

Simultaneity can only be experienced in the Here-and-Now, a very special space where everything is available and where actual life happens. Everything that was ever created, and all future ideas and perspectives are contained in that space. That space is not brief and volatile, but can be individually expanded to become your place of power, and your source of inspiration.

Linear time can be expanded and shrunken, increased and reduced. You will have to handle these rules based on your personal discretion, in order to avoid becoming its playing piece.

Sense of Proportion

This means being aware of the proper proportion of things. What is the right proportion, however? The increase of energy will strongly increase the "right proportion" for you. You will gain a view of new territories. You will face new laws that demand learning processes and adjustments from you, but that will free you from old, rigid paradigms that kept you hemmed in. The limiting veil that used to separate you from multidimensional life is now gradually dissolving. Your sense of proportion has to gradually adjust to this new view of things, permitting and processing new perspectives that are still considered unconventional now.

Harmonisation of polarities will release plenty of energy that is now able to unfold in the multidimensional space. You will discover Earth in its multidimensional facets. This will be a new, fascinating field of study for you that will bring you closer to the cosmos and its laws as well. The fascination that you have for your planet, its task in space, and with its neighbours, will let you understand why you have chosen to incarnate here, and what soul-motivation drove you.

The scope of things is a relative term that you will soon become greatly aware of. Upheavals of your previous perception will be the consequence of this. That means that you will have to adjust, but that your everyday lives here on Earth will become much easier to manage. Many paths are known to lead to the target, but it is nice to have the path made easier and unnecessary detours pointed out. Innovations in technology, your growing awareness, and greater perspective will help you develop skills that will amaze you. Humans will develop skills of great importance, helping raise their societies onto a higher evolutionary status. Harmonisation of the polarities will strongly support this development, since negative excesses are no longer possible. Everything will happen in a balanced framework instead. This will generate a great energy growth that can be used elsewhere.

The gate into the Fifth Dimension is close. You can already feel the new energy strongly. It will carry you through the last stage and support you. Many desired changes will come true in a relatively brief period of time, giving you the courage to continue on this path full of trust. Your sense of proportion will adjust to the new situation, well aware that this is a greater evolutionary step.

Great tests of courage and strength will no longer be necessary. You will be carried by this wave of energy. It will flush you into the higher dimension. Therefore, it is particularly important that you do not cling to the old. The flow of that strong energy would weaken you needlessly.

This dimensional change is comparable to a tidal wave. Surfing on that force is enjoyable. The new banks are in view and waiting for you. Full of energy, you will design your new lives there in harmony with the whole.

The dimensional change happened at the winter solstice in December 2012 for Earth. The increase of energy, however, has been accompanying you for quite a while, and is still continuing. Its intensity will slowly reduce. Around the year of 2025, you will reach the energy level you need, and have gotten used to the new laws.

A time of great learning, as well as great adjustments is ahead of you. Innovation and creativity will accompany and support you. New Earth with her people will create their Golden Age!

The community of your galactic cosmic siblings will accept you and cosmic exchange will commence.

The Legacy of Love

The source of us all, our creator goddess, our creator god, is Love itself. We are all manifested sparks of that source. It does not matter where we are in the different universes: our mission or our motivation is guiding the Love of our creator into physical manifestation, from the highly-vibrating dimensions to the lowest ones. Everyone comes from the divine source and tries to contribute to it in this manner. The divine source is not subject to polarity. It is entirely one with the whole. We are all part of that source and contribute our experiences. We develop our learning processes under many different conditions. In strongly polarised conditions, in harmonised polarities, or in integrated worlds. In part, we submerge deeply in very dense matter, as well as in the ethereal kind. There is a great range of possible manifestations. All of these manifestation sparks, however, maintain a connection to the source itself. We are all, forever and eternally, connected to our creator god, our creator goddess. That divine connection nurtures and supports us on our journey of experience.

That explains the divine yearning that rests in all of us, and our memory of unity.

Every universe develops one aspect of love to perfection. In our universe, it is the facet of love that we call compassion. Compassion is the motivation of all star-born to help, support, and teach other. That is, among other things, the reason for many space travels and the exchange among the cosmic siblings.

The current increase of the energy vibrations will soon let you participate in this loving exchange, and collect new experiences that will enrich the source.

First, you will live that love among each other here on Earth. That means that you will help, support, and teach others. You will contribute that cosmic love everywhere on the planet Earth in order to create a peaceful, loving humanity.

You will bring many different aspects of compassion to mankind because you will apply that compassion to yourself. Loving yourself unconditionally is likely one of the greatest challenges that you are now facing and that you will master. Your deep essence will now be flushed to the surface and change you, as well as your environment. You will lay the foundations for the new era and you are truly cosmic masters. The future generations will revere you as pioneers and be deeply grateful for your commitment, your courage, and your perseverance.

Love in all its facets will become part of Earth, to nourish all populations everywhere.

Harmonisation of the polarities will get rid of armed conflict, freeing plenty of energy in order to allow your further spiritual development; your multidimensional heritage will give you access to higher-dimensional levels from where your perspective can strongly expand. You will increasingly perceive that Love is the energy that keeps everything in the cosmos together, from the atom to the stars, galaxies, and universes. Love is much more than just an emotion. It is the purest energy that keeps everything together, that feeds you energetically and that you can work with. It can be used as an energy for transport, lighting, movement, etc. The universe is filled with this energy. It is free of charge and openly available, the more energy you need, the more energy will flow in, our creator goddess, our creator god, is, after all, the source of all existence.

You are part of that deity. That makes you co-creators in action. Our source is Love itself. That makes us sparks of love that implement the divine vision and make it manifest.

Love is inside you. You do not need to find it on the outside. That means that god is inside yourselves, and part of you! We are all connected to each other, no matter where in the cosmos we are located. The legacy of Love is the reason for all of our manifestations. It is our eternal hearth, our home. Separation is an illusion that will dissolve. We are all connected in the ONE. We are part of the ONE and its creation.

Let love flow. Open your chakras and your cells to let your bodies fill with that energy. That way, you will also be able to pass on that love. It will nourish yourselves first, in order to then continue to flow in affluence and enrich your environment.

Manifested love will turn this planet into the Garden of Eden that you desire.

Part of the Whole

Since everything is connected to each other, we are always part of the whole. It is like a chain: the stronger its links, the stronger the chain is as a whole. Even the strongest chain will tear if one of its links is weak. The support that you are now given by your cosmic siblings and the spiritual world must be seen in that context. The individual links cannot develop further without including the weaker ones as well. The whole is always in the process of further development. The individual parts will be involved in this. That means that no single part can ever evolve without also influencing and promoting the other parts. Concerning Earth, that means that as one person's consciousness develops, transforms their negative patterns, and permits Light to flow into their bodies, they will influence their environment and the entire planet. Every individual is, therefore, fully responsible and can influence and steer the fates of your planetary society.

The parts that belong to the source, or the ONE, have set out on a journey of experience that will allow further redevelopment of the whole. We are all co-creators in the great dance of our god, of our goddess, and bear the corresponding responsibility. We all also enjoy this all-love that permeates, embraces and nurtures us, however. We are all one. Only part of us is manifested. The yearning and memory of the unity will appear more and more in your unconscious minds. The veil that separated you is now gradually dissolving.

Harmonisation of the polarities will support this process, since the tension between the poles reduces and energy is liberated in order to develop further spiritually.

The whole, creation, nurtures and develops further through its parts – its soul parts – that are being manifested. Many different learning processes in many different dimensions contribute to this.

We are all part of creation, and thereby co-creators. We are part of the ONE, our creator god, our creator goddess. That origin, that source, is present in all of us. The search for the divine cannot be found on the outside. Accept your divinity, your co-creatorship, and create your environment in this sense. The Elohims of Earth will help the planet consciously take her place in the universe, and help design the cosmic fates.

The learning processes that are now being managed on Earth will cause the whole to ascend. Evolution of creation progresses, and Light radiates into the atomic structure. Every part of the whole is involved in this. All parts of the whole will shine in this new quality.

All of our hearts are brimming with life energy. With great respect and gratitude, your cosmic siblings are thinking of the souls currently incarnated on Earth that are helping design this evolutionary step with their personal dedication.

The Ability to Be

The challenges that you are currently going through force you to go into rest and stillness from time to time, in order to master your everyday lives again thereafter with new strength. Those downtimes are a wonderful opportunity to come closer to yourselves, and to explore your potentials and excavate your inner treasures. Everyone is carrying a long tradition inside themselves that they have acquired in the course of many incarnations on Earth and in other parts of the universe. Rest and stillness will now lead them through the increase of energy to their talents. In such moments, they will be able to consciously connect to their divinity and to achieve a higher perspective of things. This retreat into unity will enable them to powerfully master their everyday lives, and to follow their path into the Light.

In the state of being, they will experience the energy permeating them more consciously. The polarities are harmonised, and they can achieve access to their problems on the outside without valuation. They have, in a way, been part of a higher vibrational octave already in this condition, and can let the insights developed influence their lives. The body can be fully energised in such moments, and liberate itself from its burden. This is a process of healing that is routed into every cell and every atom. Conscious access to your microcosm will strengthen your bodies and enable them to fully integrate the higher vibrations. The more Light particles you can absorb into your bodies, the more healthy and vital they will be and the better you will be equipped with the challenges of this time. The preceding octave jump is an integrated process that you will continue with all your being. Your bodies are vessels, your temples, with which you are currently manifested. That body must adjust to the increased vibration, and integrate it, in order to continue, reborn, renewed in the Fifth Dimension.

In this condition of being, you will allow the cosmic energies full access to your microcosmos. Your personal emissions will increase and the dark inside you will change. This will be integrated healing and a symbiosis of bodies and spirit.

You can call this status of existence again and again in your everyday lives. Remember the emotions that you experience then, the inner images, the vibration, in order to spontaneously invigorate your everyday lives and solve issues. That inner rest and relaxation will permit integrated procedures for everyday problems and strengthen your immune system.

Many different meditation techniques, but also things such as walks and contemplations in nature, will bring you calm and stillness. Everyone will have their very personal way of finding rest. They should follow that, rather than going by external reference. Every person is a separate universe with great experience. That experience will guide and lead them. Trust in yourselves and in your potential.

All the Light particles integrated from humans will help the planet Earth in her evolution. Together, you will reach the gate into the Fifth Dimension and move on in symbiosis. The radiance of Earth and her humans will shine far into the cosmos, reaching the necessary vibrational amplitude to connect to the galactic federation and to help design the universe. Your personal contribution is, therefore, an important step in this process. It will develop you into galactic citizens. The increase of Light particles in your bodies will turn you into multidimensional beings and let you understand your origins. You are the cosmic seed that has mastered this strong Third- and Fourth-Dimensional experience together with Earth and that is now about to return home.

It is a masterpiece! The hallelujahs of your cosmic siblings will fill space, gods in manifestation and movement! My love embraces you in gratitude. Nothing matches this great achievement, it is the result of development steps that took place in the course of millennia. Maybe you can now understand our participation and unlimited love for residents of Earth. Every human who integrates the Light particles into their bodies will contribute to this result and perform their primary incarnation with us on Earth. A long-winded process is nearing its end. A new chapter can be opened, with new paradigms and new learning processes. This new era will no longer take place isolated from the cosmic neighbours, but together with your cosmic siblings, in a community of the interstellar society.

Welcome home, in the community of love that you are part of. So may it be.

Flashes of Insight

The increase of the vibration of Earth and your bodies will open new insights and ideas to you that have slumbered deeply inside you and in Earth. These insights are now flushed to the surface and will change your societies and yourselves. You are now moving into more Light-filled times, which will require new, innovative models that design your everyday lives. Difficult, narrowing traditions and rituals will be replaced and give way to fitting models compatible with the new vibration. Those new insights will reach the population of the Earth globally and bring about quick changes. The reactionary forces will be able to stand less and less against the innovations, since they will also understand that they are fighting a losing battle. Their old, encrusted and partially patriarchal rules and ideas have become obsolete. They will no longer find any fertile soil. Claims to power and possession that refer to long traditions will not find any footing at all. Re-ordering of your societies is ahead. It will be a new society, built by responsible citizens who accept their love for Earth and their fellow humans as their leading theme. The more Light Earth and her population integrates, the easier and more harmonious life will be on this planet. Great upheaval will result for everyone. Those upheavals will, however, make your lives on Earth simpler and enable you to recognise the meaning of your lives and to live accordingly. The more the heaviness recedes, the more harmonious polarities will be, and the more energy will be released for your development.

Development processes that used to take decades or even centuries will manifest and persevere in the upcoming years. This will be a challenge for everyone, since they have to adjust to new realities repeatedly. At the same time, they feel the new ease and, through their inner attitudes, can accept what is new. They instinctively recognise that it is compatible and can flow along with the new, high energies.

Many innovations have already happened in the last century. Their cadence is increasing drastically now in order to be congruent with the vibration level that will soon have the amplitude of ascension.

The frequency of energy that reaches Earth will continue to increase after the ascension into the Fifth Dimension, thereby giving you the opportunity to integrate and implement this. You have reached a new energy level that develops further. During that time, you are laying the foundations for human community on Earth, for the next generations to build on. Incredible creativity characterises the current generations. You are specialists in dimensional change. Your incarnation was not by chance. It was part of the divine plan. Accept the motivation for your incarnation and your task. It is in integration of Light in your body and in your lives, no matter what you are doing, and wherever you are. The consequence of this process is the change of Earth, and of your societies.

As the energy increases, new, creative approaches to the strategies for change are continually necessary. In the near and farther future, you will be unable to rest on what you have achieved already, but you will continue to attentively work on creation of your paradise with New Earth. The flashes of insights from your inventories will enrich and transform your societies and Earth. Let those insights rise up in you. Give them the opportunity to manifest in your lives. Accept your multidimensional existence and heritage and act accordingly. Be divine co-creators in action! Earth is yearning for her populations that awaken into new reality and accept their heritage. Take your cosmic path into Light together.

Co-Creation in the New Dimension

I have already described your contribution to this important dimensional change. It is extraordinarily important that you become aware of your contributions. Only that way can you choose and control the right steps in your lives and in your everyday work. The effects on your personal lives, your environments and your societies will show you. The process of dimensional change starts inside every individual and then radiates into their environment. Every transformation that you strive for and master will affect the whole, since we are all one in the ONE. Transformed, liberated personalities will ascend into the Fifth Dimension and found a new human society on Earth. All humans contain the memory of paradise inside themselves, which they can now call up and implement. The increased vibration, harmonisation of polarities, change of laws of nature and the newly developed societal paradigms will enable them to create that paradise on Earth anew. Your co-creatorship will find everything in its multidimensional inventory that you need to make life on Earth fulfilling, loving, and rich. Your creative ideas will no longer be limited, and their implementation will be easy. Many innovations are still impossible to imagine in the current dimension, since they need a certain vibrational frequency in order to become real.

You are now growing rapidly into the next-higher dimension. Flowing along and keeping up are your mottos now. You will become increasingly aware of how the situation is changing, how life on Earth can be made simpler and more effective for the good of the whole. The more you become aware of your co-creatorship, the more you will participate in creation of the New Earth and make your personal contributions. Dedication to the project "New Earth" will fill you and unification of all populations will touch you most deeply. This society will bring about incredible achievements. This will make your planet a jewel and her humans divine co-creators and masters.

Co-creatorship means attracting and creating things in one's personal life that serve oneself, and therefore also the whole. Negative, egotistical goals won't stand any chance of survival since they no longer receive any supporting energy. They will dissolve. The higher a person vibrates, the more harmonious their needs and wishes will be. This harmony will be the foundation for future innovations and achievements. They are the prerequisite for a new era, a new community on Earth and the cosmos.

You are still in the preparation phase for the octave jump at this time. You must get used to the increase of energy and the changes that they cause in yourselves and in your society. Over time, you will be able to master your everyday lives more and more stably, and have more capacity for your co-creatorship. You will learn to handle your thoughts: to bundle them in order to achieve your goals. You will also learn to handle your emotions in order to lead them into a positive, furthering direction. Your reason and your feelings will merge in your hearts in order to activate your co-creatorship from your symbiosis. The energy of the heart is the basic component of the Light worlds that support divine planning and drive evolution. That energy of the heart will bring peace to Earth and fully nurture mankind. The resulting properties will let mankind ascend and let you take the place that is intended for you in the Light worlds. Your co-creatorship will also expand to the cosmos, where you are involved in the plan of creation together with your cosmic siblings. Spiritual and physical wisdoms work together for the ONE. This interaction has always been reality. However, you will become more and more aware of this in the course of your awakening. This development of consciousness will allow you to better target and achieve the shared goal by your interactions, while fully integrating the holistic prospect.

The spiritual and physical worlds have various laws that can, however, create great achievements and relationships in a symbiotic relationship. You will experience and design the material and ethereal consciously, since you are divine co-creators. The Love of the ONE radiates into your creation and gives evolution the momentum it needs. Participation of all co-creators lets the evolutionary spiral grow more and more for the glory of the ONE.

New Earth

For a long time, Earth has been in the shadow of Light. There were some larger Light waves reaching Earth from time to time, feeding her residents, but life on Earth was difficult and hard. With the current dimensional change, more and more Light is flushed onto Earth, considerably changing the planet and its mankind. Rebirth of Earth and her people in a higher octave of existence has now been initiated and will soon take place. Earth and her residents are moving further and further towards the Light on their evolutionary spiral. They will merge with the worlds of Light. That process, which has been becoming evident for decades and centuries, and that is currently in its last phase, has activated many learning processes and changed Earth and mankind slowly, but steadily. Soon, Earth will have reached the vibrational amplitude where it can make its dimensional change. This ascension into an entirely new dimensional quality and the resulting adjustment is a challenge for Earth and her residents that it masters every day. After a certain time of adjustment, it will, however, learn to live with this new, high vibration and make creative contributions.

Mankind will learn to play with that vibration, try out its qualities and experience its lack of borders. A new time/space structure is disclosed that will lead them into the cosmic dance of the Light worlds and show them how the whole in which they can unfold belongs together.

The upheavals required for this are underway and will still be accelerated. The increased vibration will show you how to make your lifestyles easier in implementation of everyday matters and in targeting your goals. This will strengthen your trust in this process and bring about your dedication. This dedication will allow you to flow with this Light current in order to be in the right place at the right time, to practice your creativity and to feel embedded in the greater whole. It will give you security in a restless time characterised by changes.

In contrast to Old Earth, New Earth will go through several greater changes in order to be ready to go on its higher-dimensional path. Its matter will integrate the high-energy Light particles and fertilise the cosmos with its new radiation. The "New Earth" event will penetrate cosmic space deeply and invigorate and nourish it with new experiences. What is happening now on Earth has not seen its like in the cosmos before: a planet of the Third- and Fourth-Dimensional density that switches into a Fifth-Dimensional vibration with its residents. You chose the motivation and consent of mankind to go on this dimensional change with Earth a very, very long time ago. You have now reached the time of fulfilment. This truly is a great experiment for the divine soul shares that have incarnated here and to get through them with a free will. Free will is the highest law on Earth. It supports and influences your individual attitudes and lives. This evolution of mankind was chosen and executed by the humans directly. This unique enterprise will bring you the greatest respect and recognition of your cosmic siblings. You will contribute this treasure of experience in the divine plan of creation and enrich the whole. The currently incarnated divine soul shares deliberately bring mankind and Earth back into the lap of the cosmic family. Reunited, in the Love of our source, we will continue all together on our path along the evolutionary spiral into the Light.

The love of your cosmic siblings has accompanied you for a long time. Their help had to remain limited, however, since they were not allowed to violate your law of free will. They were only allowed to give you advice and their love. Soon, you will face them consciously and embrace them. A long path home is behind you. The table will be filled to brimming and you will be able to participate in the cosmic wealth.

This wealth from which you were separated will connect to the terrestrial matter, i.e. with your bodies.

Deficiencies and poverty will disappear from your planet. Plenty will gradually merge with Earth and with yourselves. That wealth is not only physical, but all-encompassing. Cosmic Love will fully penetrate Earth, feed its mankind in an integrated manner, and remove all deficiencies. This will create entirely new structures, e.g. in the working or commercial world, etc. Many old paradigms of life will be removed, and new ones will be created, resting on a higher-vibrational basis and with a multidimensional character. Multidimensionality will start out with a Fifth-Dimensional vibration quality. You can imagine this like a large funnel that aspires cosmic abundance, brings it onto the Fifth-Dimensional platform and distributes it there. Earth and her people will first recover from their deficiencies and then gradually integrate this wealth that is simultaneously flushed into Earth now with the high cosmic vibration. For that wealth to take its place, you need to resolve your old patterns and blocks in order to make space for something new. Be open to innovations and let go of limiting opinions and ideas. You can only take in the wealth that you allow. As mentioned, you are responsible here on Earth. You make the decisions!

This cosmic abundance is the Love of our source, of creation itself.

In December 2012, Earth reached the vibrational frequency and entered the next-higher dimensional density. The vibration frequency had been increasing for years, reaching the necessary amplitude at that time. This high vibration is similar to a raging river that powerfully floods your countries when the rivers rise after long rain. That condition will continue for a few years, until about 2025. After that, the transition time will be replaced by a more moderate rhythm. After that phase, you will have definitely reached the Fifth Dimension and gotten used to the changes produced.

Adjustment of Earth to the new dimension will be completed and humans will have finished their transformations. You will live with new impressions and adjust to the high energy. Everyone will have to tackle entirely new learning experiences, since the old paradigms will dissolve. You cannot rely on old experience, but will have to try to handle that high energy and to restructure your society. Dedication to that high energy will help you stand in the Here-and-Now in order to create something for the future. Only integrated approaches will be viable. They, however, will become matters of course for you. Your female and male shares will contribute to creation of New Earth in harmony together. Your multidimensional heritage will be available to you and the energy loss by strong polarity will be overcome. The laws of nature will adjust to the high vibration and force you to change your manner of thinking. Everyday life on Earth will be revolutionised in an unprecedented manner. The next years will, accordingly, be an incredible growth phase on your evolutionary spiral. Mankind will turn into conscious cosmic co-creators. They will become cosmic citizens of Light who are consciously reunited with their cosmic families to design the universal fates together with them.

You will barely believe what you will find inside you and what you are capable of. You will be reborn into a new level of being. Mankind is moving towards its prime, and Earth, your wonderful home, with it. The entire potential of an adult mankind is at your disposal, in combination with the cosmic forces that you may now use.

This period of growth will, of course, also have great effects on the spirituality of people. As mentioned already, you are divine sparks in action. Part of yourselves is always connected to our creator. Your inner yearning for unity, for God, will now be strengthened by the high energy. You will once again return to the divine share in yourselves. You will become aware of your divinity and contribute this understanding in your everyday lives. The resulting societal changes are clear. Divine Love will embrace Earth through you, to create humane situations. Humans will be at the centre of your achievements, always for the good of your planet Earth. Spiritual development of mankind will turn Earth into paradise in the next few centuries. The residents of Earth will live in cosmic harmony and contribute their divine co-creatorship for the good of unity, and expand and enlarge divine diversity.

The new cycle into which you are now entering is truly the prime of this planet and her mankind. Earth will become a jewel in the cosmic dance, and her radiance will be felt even in the farthest corners of space. Arts and sciences will achieve unimagined development. Your hard learning processes of the past and your commitment in the new dimension have taught you a great scope of experience with which you can support many cosmic siblings in space. You are development pioneers of a special category. You have included divine Love in your evolutionary plan. You have deliberately chosen the path of Light, and not shied back from any effort for it.

It is with great admiration that we support you on this path. Our hearts are united now and our joint journey into the Light is our future. Light and Love will guide us into all eternity.

The Milky Way and our universe are made stronger and more radiant by the ascension of Earth – and our source is enriched.

From the Viewpoint of Your Cosmic Siblings

Earth is a Fourth-Dimensional planet located at the edge of the Milky Way. The Milky Way is a huge galaxy that houses innumerable planetary systems, nourished by a centre. That centre is like a maternal being that feeds her children with her energy, takes care of them, and supports them. The solar system in which Earth is moving is now strongly attracted by the galactic centre and prepared for energetic ascension. That ascension is not only affecting Earth, but also the planets of her solar system, as well as her sun. The time has now come to give this group the place intended for it. That means that it will move closer to the centre and be exposed to higher galactic energies. This process has caused great changes on Earth and is now lifting up the planet into the Fifth Dimension, a dimension that is not comparable to the known dimensional qualities.

This ascension process is known to your cosmic siblings. They have been observing it for quite some time, trying to help and support Earth and her mankind – always under consideration of free will on Earth. All cosmic residents of Light share one quality – a loving heart for creation and the diversity of its residents. Even though that diversity manifests in vastly different bodies, its heart quality is consistent and connected to our creator god, our creator goddess.

Its quality of existence embodies the Love of our source for creation and causes it to live, pass on, and teach love in all of its facets. You can find these teachings in your old scriptures, mythologies, and antique buildings.

With great joy, the festivities for the ascension of Earth into the Fifth Dimension are currently being prepared. This ascension can no longer be prevented by the forces of darkness. Mankind has chosen this ascension and the path into Light. It is now getting ready to climb the last steps in order to once again take over its multidimensional heritage and return to the cosmic family. The experiment Earth is moving into a higher level with new challenges. This time, you will master your learning processes as partners with your cosmic siblings. The isolation of Earth will be removed by your own insights. With the high-vibrational energies, you will become aware of the illusion of separation. Harmonised polarities will contribute as well, giving the people of Earth peace and serenity. These qualities will reappear from the depths of your memories, but can now be put into practice. Many old memories from your cosmic times will motivate you and give you the scope of your projects.

Your cosmic memories will surface bit by bit now. You will feel that you had other incarnations in the cosmic space before, and that you have lived based on different laws before, those feelings will become more specific now, opening the gates of your mental bodies that have been held captive in the density of the current Earthly dimension. Your limitation will dissolve and enable you to move into vast space, where you will face cosmic dimensions. That process requires you to be connected well to Mother Earth. She gives you the stability and protection to venture into the cosmic space. That anchor will give you the courage and strength to break your limits and target new things.

Your cosmic siblings know about this process. They will only contact you once you have achieved stability on New Earth. They love you and only want the best for you. This extra-terrestrial exchange with your neighbours is to serve the whole, in order to allow you to continue on your evolutionary journey as partners. As mentioned, that process begins in the innermost of every individual, in order to then focus on Earth. Accept your premonitions and allow this process. This is an effect of the high vibrations that now reach Earth. Ascension of the vibrational frequency of Earth will break your limitations in all matters. The ethereal worlds will also be disclosed to you. Your evolutionary journey moves towards the integrated aspect of Earth. Your interaction with elves, devas and gnomes will move out of the realm of fairy-tales as you will consciously cooperate with them for the good of Earth. Their help in the creation of New Earth is most important. They know the matters of Earth. They are her specialists. Humans will learn a lot from them, and understand Earth better.

Contact with cosmic siblings, as well as earth spirits, will always be non-verbal, on the level of the heart. You will contact them telepathically. This is a romance on a high level. You will understand their wishes and needs with a loving attitude, and be able to contribute accordingly.

The development of your heart quality and the need to go into silence will give you the platform for this cooperation. Feel your environment with that sense already, and try to meet it on the level of the heart. What do the plants and trees have to tell you? What information is provided by a place of power? What vibrations can you feel there? What vibrations do you feel in your home? Why are you comfortable in one place, but not in another? All of these are questions that you will find answers to if you ask about them. The dimension of the earth spirits has always been present. However, only children and those sensitives have been able to perceive it. This is too bad, since they are part of your Earth and have supported you. Conscious cooperation on your side would help you and Earth resume a balance.

The law "as above, so below" refers to the earth spirits. Similar to your cosmic siblings, they, too, have diverse manners of expression and bodies. You will meet them both on the level of the heart. They are both not separated from you. They work together with you to unfold the Light. They are part of our source and our creator god, our creator goddess.

Dissolution of your mental limitations will gradually let you recognise the diversity of creation, enjoy it, and engage in mutual exchange. The abundance of our creator will be fully available to you. You are part of that abundance, part of the source, conscious cosmic co-creators.

Your cosmic siblings can see the labour of humans. They also know about the process you are going through, however, and its results. They do not assess and evaluate, but meet you with unconditional love. They can follow the awakening of a great part of mankind. Their joy about the growth of consciousness of the residents of Earth is great. Planet Earth is already vibrating more highly by integration of Light deeply inside matter. It will soon radiate the amplitude of ascension. The spiritualisation of matter is advancing, giving Earth and her residents a special radiance that can be perceived very well from space. The unique event of ascension onto a higher octave of existence gives Earth and her people conscious access to the cosmic space and their cosmic siblings. Separation is in the past, and the unity will be recognised and practiced on Earth. Multidimensionality will become a real term that can and will be implemented. Earth will become a new platform, travelling and exploring space in cooperation with your galactic neighbours. This Earth is committed to divine creation, continually refining, and expanding the integration of Light. The joint cosmic dance is now continued with Earth in the Love of the source of us all.

The millennia of separation are past! Very soon, we will celebrate the exchange of love together. Our expectations are high, and our love is without limits! Welcome home, at the bosom of your cosmic family, your origin.

Measure of All Things

Right now, you should still give yourself priority in your lives. That has nothing to do with egotism, but with observing your processes and transformations that present and need to be resolved in this late phase before ascension, either still or once again.

Even if you believe that you have already resolved certain patterns, they may resurface again because very deep layers of your minds are still burned by them. The high Light particles that you integrate now are like centrifuges. They dissolve negative patterns and bring them to the surface in order to be processed. Boldly face such negative subjects, and resolve them definitively now. Relief will be your reward, connected to a liberated physical feeling of resurrection. The ascension ahead of you will be a rebirth in a new octave of existence that will not permit any old and negative patterns. Your bodies will be renewed, refined, and spiritualised by this ascension.

The Fifth Dimension will bring spiritualisation of matter with it. All matter will charge with Light, and its density will be changed. Therefore, the laws of nature known to you will change based on density. You are being gradually prepared for this, and your technologies and behaviours will need to be adjusted accordingly; there will be a great process of re-learning. Believe me: everything will become simpler. First, you need to get used to what is new: multidimensionality, non-linearity; new density of matter, and harmonisation of polarities. These are only key words for you right now. Soon, you will be working with them, and revolutionise your lives on Earth.

There is no need to fear those changes. The energy levels will change quickly, but still gradually, until it stabilises on a certain level to then increase at a more moderate pace. This phase of transition into the Fifth Dimension will likely be the most difficult thing, since you will continually have to deal with the present energy level and adjust to it.

Therefore, I urgently advise you to take repeated breaks during this chaotic time, to let you integrate that high energy into your bodies. That will give you the time to listen to its signals and to access your potential. That potential is your inventory of talents that you have developed throughout your incarnations. It will once again be available to you now. You can activate it. Ask your innermost, your divine self about it. It will reactivate the talents you need now, and provide them for your use; do you want to paint, write, make music, or speak before an audience, etc.? Your inventory will surely contain a life where you have learned and exercised that talent. If you go into stillness, to your centre, you can have this conversation with your divine self, and allow it to guide you.

The search for answers in your innermost, rather than on the outside, is a great challenge. Your innermost is a veritable treasure trove that belongs only to you and that only you can open and use.

The measure of things is love for yourself and for All-That-Is. Love for yourself is likely the most difficult thing. It requires you to accept yourselves as you are, to forgive yourselves and to be patient with yourselves. You must give yourselves the space you need to stand by yourselves. This is incredibly difficult in hectic times, since this inner search for yourself will need those breaks I have already mentioned. Do not seek love on the outside. It is only illusion. Someone who loves themselves will experience the ecstasy they are looking for. A partner will then no longer have to fill a vacuum. If you learn to unconditionally love yourselves, you are also ready to pass on that love. Your entire personality will radiate that love. It makes you strong and invulnerable. You will become the I AM. Unconditional love for yourselves originates in your divinity and connects you to the source of all existence.

The increase of the energy fluctuations will help you develop that love for yourselves and for All-That-Is. The incarnated divine sparks will turn Earth into the desired Garden of Eden and your mission on Earth will be complete.

Mission on Earth for Currently Incarnated Souls

Many people who are currently incarnated on Earth in this time of transition are closely familiar with this planet. They have helped characterise its fate for millennia. Many souls were motivated to incarnate here in order to help Earth and her residents to develop into the Light – and to anchor divine Love on the planet. Since the beginning of time, you have striven, incarnation by incarnation, to manifest that Love on Earth. You have accepted great efforts and are now able to celebrate the completion of your mission on Earth. Earth has become very dear to you in this long time. She is your home now. You arrived as cosmic seed. You will decide whether you want to return to your origin among the stars, or whether you prefer to incarnate on Earth again after your successful mission. As specialist for evolution, you have done your best. Recognition of your achievements will sound loudly through space. You have supported Earth and her residents in great, difficult learning processes. You have paved the way with your love. You have done pioneering work that demanded a lot from you and that required a high price from you at times.

My dear readers, those times are soon over. Soon, you will be recognised for what you are. Your commitment will be rewarded. You will master resurrection into the Fifth Dimension and open this gate for many people. You are the pioneers for this generation, its supports, and an example for it.

Some achievements will be born from your initial ignition. New paradigms will be created, and the expansion of Light will be supported; you will know that the basic motivation of all your incarnations will be implemented and you will celebrate anchoring of divine Love on Earth. You will be able to look back onto your cycle on Earth with great gratitude as you now achieve your mastery. That mastery will return you to the cosmic bosom from which you chose to be separated in order to help design the experience on Earth and to guide mankind onto the higher octave of existence. Past labour is dissolved. You continue on your path on Earth and in the cosmos as conscious, divine particles of Light. Your limited perception is a thing of the past. Your connection to All-That-Is has become reality. You are the merger of divine Light particles in the ONE and at the same time individual beings in action. You will become part of the conscious heavenly hosts that work to praise the ONE.

You are co-creators in the universal divine plan. You have progressed into the densest matter and you have helped it transform into a higher octave of existence.

Everyone carries the blueprint inside, using their female shares for this. The femininity that is inherent in everyone will now be reactivated and put into practice by the male share. Femininity will once again take its due place on Earth, support the process of rebirth, and create New Earth. Harmonisation of polarities will make this a cooperative partnership, or a co-creatorship on a new level of existence. Try to express your female shares. Let this great potential rise to the surface. This ascension into the Fifth Dimension is an integrated process. All of your shares are needed now. All of your talents will be used for the good of the whole, the good of mankind, and the good of Mother Earth. A renewed, responsible mankind in possession of all its talents will continue the journey through the cosmos with the spaceship Earth and further climb the spiral of Light.

The Way Out

As mentioned before, humans with long Earthly experience are currently living on Earth. They have a special motivation of love for Earth and mankind. Not all people living right now fall into this category. Many souls incarnated on Earth based on different motivations. Earth offers strongly polar, Third- and Fourth-Dimensional experience processes with free will. Many souls chose these learning processes in order to increase their experience. Of course, those people are also cosmic in origin. Their feelings of home for Earth are not as sustainable, however, they may feel like strangers on Earth and have difficulty living with this density and the corresponding laws on Earth.

Some of them have only come to experience the learning processes in this phase of ascension. The quality of their motivation gives them the order or the obligation to help design and support this ascension, or to deal with their own matters only.

The drastic ascension of energy in this time of transition will lead many souls to prefer to leave this planet in order to acquire further learning elsewhere. This decision must be made individually by each soul. Each soul has its own motivations for what experiences it wants to get to know. Those who remain behind always find it hard to let go of one of theirs. However, be aware that you are, really, always staying connected, even though your physical density will make it seem differently. We are all one. Separation is an illusion of your Third- and Fourth-Dimensional density. You will soon recognise this by the further ascension of vibrational quality on Earth. Death is merely a metamorphosis into a different reality of existence. The love you emanate, the love that you feel for the deceased, knows no dimensional borders. It radiates through all levels of existence, from the densest matter to our source. You are connected to your ancestors and deceased in love at all times, which can support you on your developmental path. As you can see, the heart quality breaks all borders. This will be the basis for your cohabitation on Earth and in the cosmos in the new, Fifth-Dimensional reality. Love for yourselves and for others will be the driving force of your future actions on Earth and in space.

The way out into different learning experiences and reliabilities of being is only a transfer to a different cosmic school or playground. Death only refers to your physical hull. You are immortal, and always connected to our creator god, our creator goddess. Your learning experience will let you contribute to expansion and diversity of creation.

We are all connected and support and help each other. This is also the reason for these messages. Divine Love connects us forever. We are all one in our creator god, in our creator goddess.

The many cycles of life that you spend on a planet will characterise your DNA, your behaviour, and your appearance. These qualities are then carried to other planets where you live. This will lead to cosmic enrichment of your DNA. That is good. We are not separated from each other, and we all have the same DNA origin. It is only enriched by different learning experiences in various dimensional densities in this manner. Earth and her people completing the octave jump into the Fifth Dimension will now trigger a sort of déjà-vu in many of you. Your memory will bring up familiar feelings and potential solutions. The increased vibration and its consequences will not be foreign to you, which will facilitate adjustment. You, in turn, will be able to use your multidimensional treasure to work with. The many ethnicities on Earth, the many hair colours, the different bodies, all of that has a cosmic origin. The cosmos has a great variety of living beings. Some of them want to get to know Earth in greater detail and have become established here. The memory of your cosmic roots will give you wings and bring space closer to you. The separation you have long suffered under will dissolve. You will be able to quench your yearning for your home planet. Everything will suddenly make sense, and you will be able to understand your decision from back then. Love will return you to your origin. Since separation is an illusion, you will experience everything in the Here-and-Now.

You also experience cosmic diversity in your flora and fauna, in your buildings, in art and in science. Many people are guided by their origin. They have manifested wonderful, ingenious treasures on Earth. Even though some of them will not consciously remember, they were able to activate their DNA and to create pieces of art in all areas. The cosmic family has already been with you for eons. Very soon, we will consciously embrace each other.

The story of your home planet Earth will become accessible to you and bring you clarity. Your association to the cosmos can be understood in an integrated manner.

We are all ONE in the ONE.

Essence of Love

Divine Love permeates the entire micro- and macrocosmos. It keeps the atomic structure together. It is, in a way, the gravitational field of creation. All matter consists of the purest divine energy of Love. It is the physical expression of your creator, pulsating in their harmony. That pulse is similar to our heartbeat, conveying divinity into the physical. As a consequence, there is no dead matter. We are all part of a living creation, a living god, a living goddess. We all contribute to praising them in creation. All that is, all that ever was and all that will be comes from our divine source. All is connected and one. All of creation is filled by the divine energy of Love.

Matter is, therefore, condensed energy of Love, expression of the divine. The divine soul shares acting in creation enrich the source and expand it. Some of these divine soul shares are, for example, currently incarnated here on Earth. All of mankind is part of this deity – our creator.

In other words: everyone is divine. You will now gradually become aware of this inherent divinity that you have. It will characterise your feeling of responsibility accordingly. As a result, everyone is connected to All-That-Is. If you do anything to another, you are doing it to yourself!

The rise of vibrational frequency potentiates that energy of Love and makes it express in yourselves, in your societies, and on your planet. Mother Earth is, just like you, a divine soul share. She is a living being that expresses our creator's love and that serves as a platform for our soul shares to unfold. Feel her love for you. Together, you can contribute your love for creation, praise and enrich ITS glory.

Earth is your nourishing mother, your home. Even though you are cosmic seed, the planet on which you are currently undergoing your learning processes does become your home. Through your connection with All-That-Is, you can be incarnated on Earth and yet feel and live your cosmic roots. The essence of Love that permeates everything makes this possible. Development of your DNA will let you expand the aspects of love that you learned on other planets to Earth. Interaction of space with Earth already takes place because of this – through yourselves. You will meet a family you know well when you make your first contact with your cosmic siblings. The energy of love that will embrace you is nothing strange, but it is part of yourselves as well.

The essence Love builds the spiral of Light to the divine. Where there is no love, there is shadow. Lovelessness has a destructive effect, while Love is the building block of creation. It is the divine power that nurtures creation and keeps it alive, enables it to continue to spread and develop. The entire cosmos is an expression of our creator's Love, and we are all sparks of Love in motion.

Even though mankind is partially unaware of this fact, it is still part of this love. The next few decades will return mankind to its soul and human right and dock it there. They will remember who they are, where they come from and where they are going. They will awaken in Love and their emanations will enrich all of creation. The ecstasy of Love for All-That-Is, co-creators in the whole, the dance of dances, into all of eternity.

Mankind has been separated from these happenings multiple times for millennia. That separation will soon have definitely dissolved, and Love can complete its work on Earth.

Earth is accepted into the family of Light and will take the place there that it is due. Mankind will contribute to the heavenly events and continue to climb the spiral of Light. Divine Love expands continually. Our universe sparkles with Light in the cosmos like a high-carat diamond. The universes are blossoming in the face of God, since every individual's contribution will affect the whole! Every individual is responsible, carried, and nurtured by divine Love. This flow of Love is the essence of life for everyone.

Cosmic Knowledge

Millennia ago, various cosmic siblings settled by the River Nile, where Egypt is today, in order to bring cosmic information to Earth for founding of new civilisations. Your current western culture on Earth is mostly based on this inventory of knowledge. At the same time, other parts of Earth experienced similar visits from the stars and were taught by them. The basis of this knowledge is congruent, since it is divine in origin. Many centuries were necessary to integrate that knowledge, and many setbacks happened. Now, mankind has agreed to follow the Light and to leave darkness behind. That leads to many personal and societal transformations that you are now powerfully putting into practice. That cosmic knowledge is available to you in your holy places, pyramids, and old temples on all continents. Those holy places open your inner cosmic gates, that is: your DNA, and allow you to access your cosmic heritage. Those places are being energetically activated once more in recent decades, after a long, forced slumber, since Earth needed a certain vibrational frequency before that cosmic knowledge could be made accessible to all humans. That opening of your cosmic gates will develop you into cosmic citizens. A person with opened cosmic gates will automatically activate them in their fellow humans. That is an energetic process that serves to awaken and inform mankind as comprehensively as possible. Do not be surprised to be visited by old memories from your cosmic time, either waking or in your dreams at night.

All of your learning experiences that you have made in the cosmos are stored in your DNA. That cosmic knowledge is now available to you. Visits to holy sites in particular can open your inner cosmic gates – depending on your state of consciousness. This activation will not overwhelm you, you will be able to integrate it gradually in yourselves, and to provide it to society. This will open up new points of view for solving your issues, integrated approaches will be tackled that involve a superordinate view of the situation, and then implement it.

These ideas that you will find revolutionary come from the cosmic space that is contained inside you. Contact with outer cosmic civilisations happens through yourselves, through awakening of your multidimensional DNA, your personal genetic code. Mankind is awaking from itself to become cosmic citizens. Interstellar exchange will only happen later, once conscious mankind has integrated and implemented its own heritage. That will permit interaction as partners. The time of the gods coming from the outside is past.

Earth itself contains a lot of cosmic knowledge, since it has been made of similar components as its stellar neighbours. It is a great library of knowledge for you that will help you understand space as well. The search for the laws of life will go from the outside inwards here as well. All that you need to know is inside you, and in Earth. You will now gain a deeper understanding of the law "as above, so below", and be able to clearly understand interrelations. That hermetic law was transferred to you at the River Nile millennia ago. Your current science is about to understand that law in its full depth. What used to be a matter of faith can now be calculated and rationally explained by your scientists. You will discover the space inside space in yourselves and draw conclusions on the outside. All creatures are universes in themselves. The same laws of life apply everywhere, no matter if they are physical, mental, or spiritual. The divine energy that keeps creation alive is the same everywhere.

Depending on the dimensional density, the laws of nature differ from planet to planet. The components of life, however, come from a single source and adjust to their environment. The triangle is the basis of matter. All of creation is built on this triangulation. Evolution follows the same laws. The big pyramids show you this law of the components of life. The setup of matter is subject to a grid that creates the necessary stability to let divine energy circulate freely and the vibrations of living creation can emanate.

Your religions reflect that law as well, in the trinity, God the father, God the son and God the Holy Ghost, or Brahma, Vishnu and Shiva, etc.; all of these are aspects of unity.

Cosmic knowledge is about the basis of creation, leaving the unity and entering manifestation. Re-connection to unity is preserved while manifestation is driven and supported. The divine flow of life flows into creation this way. The manifestations become an expression of God.

Life and all that you create from it is based on this holy principle, both on Earth and in the cosmos. Clearly recognising basis of the component of life will point of unexpected opportunities for your co-creatorship and help you put them into practice.

"As above, so below" shows you the original principle of creation: life itself.

My dear residents of Earth, you are part of the cosmos and the divine expression on your wonderful planet.

The New Era

Revocation of the tension between the polarity poles will, as mentioned, harmonise your everyday lives. Lots of released energy will be available to you to build New Earth, giving more space to your creativity because you will be able to free yourselves from old laws that use to hem you in. You will have to carefully feel your way into that new freedom in order to experience yourselves holistically in a new life. Your old life experiences will become void, since the swings between the poles of polarity will be removed and continued by activation of the middle tension width. Fluctuations are, therefore, a lot lower, as is the loss of energy. The powers needed to reach a goal must be realigned now. Bundling of powers will become simpler and more efficient. Your projects will blossom almost magically for you initially, until you have gotten used to the new way of handling energy. For example, you will feel as if you are being supported by a magical guidance. Of course, that will not be the case. However, the change may have that effect on you. By getting used to this new paradigm, you will get to know it better and learn to fully utilise it. I can guarantee you:

your lives, your everyday matters on Earth, will become much simpler, calmer, and humorous.

Harmonisation of polarities will be brought about by increase of the vibrational frequency. It is a quality of the Fifth Dimension. You will be confronted with it very soon and come to enjoy it.

First, however, the polar tension will increase. There will be hard trials ahead that will challenge mankind. My dears, trust in this evolutionary process. Try to be centred as far as you can, in order to tackle what is happening on the outside and the inside without strain. This time of transition is very brief. You are nearing rebirth to the next-higher octave of existence, virtually the labour pains.

Labour pains are always hard to bear. However, they bring about the long-expected new. This expectation or that hope will give you strength in order to get through the last conflicts. Exceedingly difficult times are behind you and this path will be like child's play by comparison. The goal is close enough to touch. It will motivate you and give you the strength you need. Human consciousness is now much higher and permits more specific actions and solutions for issues. Earth has almost reached the vibrational level needed. This will make transformations of old behavioural patterns simpler and enable you to strive for integrated solutions that already contain the Fifth-Dimensional seed as a result. This time of transition is a fluent transfer into the Fifth Dimension. The higher the energy level, the more shares already belong to the next-higher octave. The Fifth-Dimensional seed is now sown so that it can develop with the increased vibrational frequency, to then be available to you after your ascension into the Fifth Dimension. Your philosophy towards life, mankind, and the planet is starting to transform. It adjusts to the higher vibration and will gradually prepare your Fifth-Dimensional everyday lives. That means the world of your thoughts is strongly changing now. This – your personal – rebirth is already happening. Soon, it is going to manifest. You will awaken into new, multidimensional humans, becoming cosmic citizens and co-creators. This is a process that you are continually bringing about. You will become physically and mentally ready to enter the dimensional gate in order to continue to grow into the new era.

It was divine intention for Earth and her humans to complete this dimensional change now. However, since the matter is Third- and Fourth-Dimensionally aligned, that transfer had to happen gradually so that matter, the human bodies, and the human minds could adjust to it. This adjustment will trigger plenty of unrest and stress on Earth, forcing people into their centre, back to their roots, into their inner-most. This is the Fifth-Dimensional preparation for your future, since the new humans will contribute to the new society from the inside out. Responsible for themselves, they will design life and society.

The energy of the heart of every human is currently undergoing strong development. That means that your hearts will be energised, and old traumas will dissolve. That process takes place on the physical, as well as the ethereal levels. Your heart is the driving force of your lives. The energy of the heart will be the basis of New Earth. Your physical hearts currently need to undergo a sort of training in order to be able to integrate the high energy. Support your hearts with the rest and relaxation you need in order to allow them to perform this important work.

A society that is based on the loving will support its humans and promote them. It will teach them to take responsibility for the whole, aware that the whole is only ever as strong as its weakest part. The "compassion" aspect of love will now be observed more strongly. This is a galactic principle that we are all committed to. The further mankind grows into the Fifth Dimension, the more mandatory the cosmic laws will be for it. The degree of consciousness of mankind will soon point out the necessary vibrational frequency and be equated to the remaining stellar civilisations. Of course, that also means that humans will take the same responsibility for the whole. This is a dedication to Love and to Light.

Harmonisation of the polarities makes it easier for you to follow the Light, since the great, old fluctuations between the poles have been revoked. Many negative expressions of love and its manifestations, such as hate, fury, jealously, etc. will disappear.

Yes, my dear people: you are entering into an entirely new era now. Love will be its driving force, as your hearts are for yourselves. Without Love, creation would dissolve. We are all part of this immeasurable divine Love, our creator, emanating it into the manifestation. We are the expression of our source. We are all ONE.

Conclusions

Studying evolution and the history of Earth, you can draw conclusions as to the present. One should learn from mistakes, unfortunately, you have not managed to do that as well as you were hoping to, no matter if in interaction with Mother Earth, nature, or with the many armed conflicts that you have gone through on your planet. You have founded some organisations that serve the good of mankind, you have built democracies, and striven to enforce humanity. All of those efforts had to be put into practice in a Third- and Fourth-Dimensional, strongly polar energy. That was a difficult project! The will of many to create a peaceful planet repeatedly failed due to this strongly polar energy. With the current ascension of the vibrational frequency of Earth and the resulting harmonisation of polarities, you will be able to implement some wishes for mankind and for Mother Earth. Drawing conclusions from your past will become more difficult, since you will be moving in a new frequency range with which you have no experience yet. The loving wishes for Mother Earth and for mankind are vibrating at a higher frequency. They will complete ascension to the Fifth Dimension with you. The destructive approaches, however, will be unable to break through the barrier of ascension. They will receive less and less energetic nutrition and are doomed to be destroyed.

Over time, you will then be able to make use of your experience. Evolution continues, and although you will soon have reached the Fifth Dimension, you still have a lot to learn. Drawing conclusions to Fifth-Dimensional events at a later time will help you continue on your evolutionary path more efficiently, since you will learn from your mistakes and not keep having them catch up with you. That is a Fifth-Dimensional aspect that will advance you speedily. Mankind will develop more quickly in future than it has been possible so far. Do not forget that everyone will be reborn into the new vibrational octave. They have had to do great transformative work before, and will gradually recognise their multidimensionality and let it flow into their lives. New paradigms will be available that no longer permit any conclusion as to Old Earth.

Your Earth will create new structures and teach mankind how to handle them. Life on Earth will become more multi-layered without any reference to old habits. Great relearning will happen and promote your creativity. Unfathomed potentials will become available for mankind and you will be thinking and acting on entirely different tracks. The increased energy will point you the way. Dedication to that energy will be the pivot there. The better you flow with that vibrational frequency, the easier your everyday lives and implementation of your projects will be. Living the present – being in the Here-and-Now – is the challenge you are facing. That was the case in the old energy already, but it is becoming unavoidable with the ascension of the vibrational frequency. Love is only happening in the Now, and only in the Now will you be happy and content. Satisfaction will flow into your future work and influence it. The Fifth-Dimensional vibrational frequency does not know linearity. Everything is present in the Now! Conclusions are, as a consequence, no longer happening in a linear attitude. The past and future will be experienced in the Now. That statement will still make you shake your heads today. As I said. Go on your path step by step into the Fifth Dimension. That way, you will be able to adjust to the new conditions. That adjustment will have to happen quickly, however. It will affect all of mankind. Everyone will be challenged to develop their place on New Earth. The increased vibrational frequency acts on your bodies and your minds so that you can integrate the Fifth-Dimensional energy. Give yourselves the rest you need to allow those mutations to happen. Perceive the signals of your bodies and your minds, and support yourselves in this process. Awaken from yourselves into the new octave of existence and welcome the new morning, the new life on your beloved planet. Together with Mother Earth, you will turn your home into a jewel, a paradise to praise creation. United with your cosmic siblings, your path will continue on the divine spiral of Light, the expression of the Love of the ONE.

End and Beginning

Omega and alpha! A long period is nearing its end.
Not only for Earth, but for your entire solar system. This
will now be freely accessible to the energies of the
galactic centre. The maternal, female energy of our
galactic centre protects, supports, and teaches Earth and
the solar system and embraces them. These are qualities
that every mother shows for her children. Like every
mother on Earth acts out of love, the same happens in
our galactic space. The female qualities that are present
in every human will undergo great development. Your
creativity will unfold physically and metaphysically,
integrated creations in all areas will be designed by you.
Harmonisation of the female and male energies will give
your ideas manners of expression that you would
consider utopian. All of your activities will contain this
maternal, galactic energy of love and accordingly
promote and support Earth and mankind. The wellbeing
of the community, both globally and privately, will be the
motto of this new time. Compassion within the family, an
aspect of divine Love, will penetrate, nurture, and
promote all projects and activities.

The new era is more than just some reformation or revolution. It is a rebirth into a new level of being. It is not based on old, conventional structures, but released from them. You will enter a new, still virginal level that will be designed by you, just as you had to relearn everything and get used to Earth after your birth. The situation will be similar in the new era, but with the difference that you will be able to access your entire potential that you have acquired in so many incarnations.

End and beginning: an end and a new beginning! You are experiencing the end to your current living conditions every day, structures in life that used to be important to you are slowly dissolving. New approaches of interaction begin to become prevalent and established. Your economy is undergoing immense restructuring, since old values cannot continue in the high energy anymore. Scandals are uncovered and force reorientation. Earth will make you see your omissions and neglect that will lead to steps essential for survival. All of your living conditions that do not serve the whole will have to be viewed and restructured, or else they will collapse. These scenarios are connected to the end of Old Earth and the beginning of the new level of existence. Fifth-Dimensional approaches in your decisions have already been developed. They will grow into the new era of Earth and continue to develop further thereafter. The end is characterised by letting go and going into the void.

The latter may be the most difficult part for humans, since it requires great trust in themselves and in life as a whole. Only in the void will you find new solutions that will take you further. Only in the void will you feel yourselves and your true needs. No matter how difficult that phase is, it contains all your wishes and plans, and it can lead to great personal creativity. It can assign you to the place that is better suitable for you. Strokes of fate are very painful but may set the tracks for an entirely new life. It will be the key to new growth and discovery. Every aspect of life has a positive and a negative side to it. Try to see the positive side in your process, and to develop it further. You are carrying so many treasures inside you that only wait to be discovered and excavated.

You have nothing to compare the vibrations of the new era on Earth to. You must feel and probe it carefully in order to develop new procedures from it for how to handle that high vibrational frequency. The feasibility of your work and projects will be determined. You will have to rethink since your old solution approaches will no longer work. Feeling that high energy will be best to help you handle that – with integrated use of all your senses.

Even though there will be some initial issues, you will be much lighter and more comfortable in that Fifth-Dimensional vibration. It will be as if a burden was taken from your shoulders. Plans and wishes will be easier to implement because the power of your thoughts can be implemented better. Thanks to the harmonisation of polarities, no loss of energy will be suffered anymore.

My dear people, as I have mentioned, you are now walking forward into this new level of existence and adjusting to this vibration. That adjustment started years ago. It will become more and more urgent now and in the new few years. Believe me that you cannot avoid this evolutionary step, but you can face that new vibrational frequency with dedication.

Trust in this octave jump and in yourselves will help you in this strongly changing time.

Your cosmic neighbours will accompany you and help you if you desire this.

Excessiveness

Harmonisation of the polarities will considerably reduce the excessiveness that you know in your societies. That affects all conditions in life in which you are embedded. Addiction and excess in all forms will no longer be possible. The high energy will no longer nurture such excessiveness, but will wash it out and cut it off. Personal needs, and those of Earth, will heal.

All effects of your deeds resonate with the whole, with Earth, her mankind, and the cosmos. The laws of the Fifth Dimension have a superordinate perspective. They serve Light and Love. Those laws will be anchored on Earth over time, replacing Third- and Fourth-Dimensional paradigms. As mentioned, they are cosmically aligned. They will determine and characterise your everyday lives on Earth. Those new laws have a much wider circle of effect than the old ones, and, following that, greater consequences. This is similar to an echo that is sounding into space. All of your thoughts and activities will be perceived as a whole.

A new growth phase is ahead of you. Be very responsible for your thoughts. Manifest them through your lives and your future. Some goals will have to be revised and find a new consensus, in particular if your projects are very long-term ones. If those projects are still rooted in the old energy, they may yet adjust to the new energy and its laws to come to fulfilment. They must, however, serve the whole, rather than being some egotistical plans for a minority. The latter stand no chance of being fulfilled, since they are not compatible with the new energy. Do not be surprised if you find that certain projects will fail while others are bound for success.

Excessiveness in all its forms will no longer exist. This, too, is an effect of harmonisation of the polarities that only permits a certain bandwidth of duality. That bandwidth is, of course, still polar, but no longer at the same scope as you had to experience it under the old energy. Polarity is harmonised, rather than being revoked. Excess is part of the greatest tension of polarity and will be revoked or resolved. You will continue to have polar learning processes, but they will be harmonised and belong to a Fifth-Dimensional vibrational frequency. New learning experiences will be the consequence. However, I promise you that they will no longer be as painful as the ones you had to experience in the old energy.

The vibrations of your hearts that originates in your divinity knows that harmonisation already. Isn't it great to design your lives and your societies in that ambience in future? Think about it and try integrating your near future in your lives already.

Many Fifth-Dimensional approaches have already reached you. They only wait to be used and to be involved in your lives and your societies. They feel good. They may still appear a bit utopian and fantastic, though. Feel them and be bold enough to break through your limits, or to at least open them. Be aware that they serve the whole and that they support your growth. Put your fears aside and boldly move on along your path into Fifth-Dimensional areas.

In your deepest heart, you are housing a vibrational frequency that is balanced when you go into stillness and rest. That frequency will let you catch a glimpse of the harmonised quality that you will soon meet. Cosmic vibrations of the galactic centre will be taken up by your hearts first and forwarded to your bodies from there. Your cells can better integrate the information sent that way, without losing any energy. Increase of this vibration leads to harmonisation of the polarities. The maternal centre of our galaxy contributes to increasing the vibrational frequency in your solar system through its vibration. Direct access to those vibrations leads the entire solar system onto a higher octave of existence. The community of your solar systems is now ready to experience the proximity of the galactic centre and to take another evolutionary step. Like Earth, all planets of your solar system and your sun are subject to great changes right now in preparation for the new energy. Earth is not an exception. All is interlinked with everything else. This pending octave jump will have its effects far into cosmic space. It will nourish your adjacent galaxies as well. The entire sector of the galaxy is involved in this change.

The Purpose of Being

The purpose of your entire incarnations on Earth and in cosmic space serves our source, our creator god, our creator goddess, whose part we all are. All practiced experience in the many different dimensional qualities leads every soul to develop into a jewel. Every experience cycle contributes to it, and the soul receives a new facet polish – figuratively speaking – until that beautiful diamond withdraws into unity for the glory of the ONE.

Sometimes, more difficult learning experiences require multiple incarnation cycles. Every life will give you a "common theme", a learning destination that you had chosen before the incarnation in order to achieve that facet polish. Some highly developed entities that have already developed a multifaceted diamond, for example, may return to Earth to anchor galactic compassion on Earth and to help and serve humans on their path. The situations chosen by you are always learning experiences of love in all of its aspects. This is love for yourself, your fellow beings and for Earth. It goes from the personal aspect to the superordinate one of divine, unconditional Love.

If you look back at the end of an incarnation cycle, you can recognise that common theme. You will find how far that facet of your diamond was polished, and whether further polishes would be needed. That way, you can determine your next incarnation. For conscious people, that insight can occur earlier in life, and determine their further path without any painful confusions and deviations. The path of life may lead to a vocation to bring divine Love closer to humans in some manner and to support them.

Every soul determines its own incarnations, since every soul is a co-creator in the ONE.

Beingness is realisation of the soul shares in an incarnation. The more soul shares can be integrated, the more fulfilled will a living cycle be designed. The incarnated entity feels close to the ONE and can contribute in its life in a more integrated manner. Those soul shares are the total of many different experiences. It is your potential that is available to you and that can be called up. Every soul chooses the bandwidth of its talents that it wants to live before incarnation. It can, however, easily call up further skills that are part of their potential. However, it can also acquire new skills and experiences that are then added to its potential. In other words: you are walking treasure chests that can create even the impossible! Withdrawing into yourselves will create the conditions in which you can open your treasure chest in order to reach your talents. You can practice activating those talents so that they will be available to you and to mankind.

In this time characterised by upheaval, you will make use of your potential and create New Earth. Everyone will do so in their personal lives, in their environments and in their societies. You are able to create new, integrated structures, to adjust to new laws and to help Earth in her healing process and to support her. That certainty comes from our source, of which we are all part. The creation potential that is present in every soul spark is now activated. The purpose of existence will accompany you creator gods/creator goddesses into a new octave of existence, a great step along your evolutionary spiral into Light.

Light will guide you, brighten up dark locations and manipulations and lead to transformation. It will point you the way, support and nurture you. Light will develop you into multidimensional beings and accompany you on your journey through space. Earth and her humans are messengers of Light, witnesses of a great transformation and teachers in this respect.

Freedom of Thought

Your mental bodies are used to thinking in certain thought tracks, depending on your association with your religions, societies, and traditions. From time to time, you will be surprised by thought flashes that do not fit into your traditional concept. You will mostly ignore those thoughts and push them aside, the increased vibration and development of your DNA will increase the frequency of those unconventional sudden ideas. They will teach you to break through your limitations in order to permit a greater perspective of your thoughts. Multidimensional thoughts will now be attracted by your spirit. You must process that mentally and emotionally. You will find that the origin of those thoughts is of superordinate relevance, while still being received by yourselves. The more you develop in multidimensionality, the more you will become like an open vessel for those thoughts. They contain the seed for the new time. You will need a time of maturation before you can put those thoughts into practice. That time of maturation permits a more integrated manner of thinking and growing beyond your old thought structures. The forms of thoughts mentioned are attracted by all people. It is a global development that will dissolve your limitations. Your soul, your divine share, will remain in multidimensionality and can better connect to you through the increase of the vibrational frequency. Cosmic information can reach you much more easily now, as can information from other humans that you can receive non-verbally. You will, in a way, feel the messages, no matter if they come from Earth or from the cosmos. They are a sort of channelling, which is the manner in which these lines are received. You must accept and integrate those new thoughts first. A new worldview will become evident for you and unconventional manifestations will become possible. Those new, generous thoughts will turn your activities into great innovations. You will manage integrated development of your societies.

The freedom of your thoughts and their lack of limitation are something you will have to get used to first, to integrate them gradually into your everyday lives. Overthrowing fears and rules, and setting out on new paths, are things that you will have to learn first. You are not alone in this process. You will find that your fellow humans are feeling similarly. That will help you change your lives. The wealth of the presented options will overwhelm you at first and teach you to go deeply inside you, in order to feel the path you wish to continue on. It is known that there are various paths to the goal. The path is what is decisive. Choose it as you feel like. Let all your senses activate and contribute in an integrated manner. A great, colourful fan of opportunities is available to you. Explore the many new games of life with courage and trust. Through your life cycle, you participate in the theatre of the world, trying to learn and play your role to the best of your abilities. That distanced approach to your lives renders many things that are difficult for you relative. It can help you make superordinate decisions. Focusing only on yourself rarely gives you good advice. A greater perspective can only be recognised from a distance.

Spontaneous inspirations or dreams are the building blocks of your new lives. Give them the space they deserve. Write them down, register them so that they can serve you at a later time. Perceive them without bias and try not to censor them. Those puzzle pieces will develop into an image that will help you proceed. Everyone has their own images, and those many different images bring about greatly creative potential of options for mankind and for Earth.

The time of abundance is arising on Earth. It is wealth in all respects, and for everyone. Enjoy living on Earth now. Contribute your potential and create the era of New Earth. This new cycle will be called the "Golden Age".

The "Golden Age" or the Rediscovered Paradise

Your mythologies and fairy tales tell about paradise and its loss. They tell about the descent into duality with all its pain and tragedy. This long period of increasingly dense energy with additional great polar tension is now gradually dissolving. The increased cosmic vibration that has been reaching you for a while has let you grow into the transition phase that will lead you to the ascension into the next-higher octave of existence. The increased vibration changes your learning processes as well. The higher the vibrational frequency, the more harmonious living conditions will be. Strongly polar learning experiences will, therefore, soon be a thing of the past. New learning experiences of a Fifth-Dimensional character are starting to reach you. One of them is handling of partnerships of any kind, dealing with time, using your bodies and matter, etc.

A new era commences with new structures that you need to adjust to. Those new learning experiences and handling of that Fifth-Dimensional energy will return you to paradise, back home where you are from. Your descent into the past density will now be revoked again by your ascension. The past learning experiences remain stored in you. They are part of your treasure of life, your potential, and will be supplemented by new ones now.

A long, dark period will soon be behind you. The farther you continue, the more Light will be available to you. Where there is Light, there also is Love. Your path will be bright and clear.

The new era into which you are now growing will be quite different from the old one. I have described a great many changes already. However, it is difficult to point out new things to you now, while you are still caught in the Fourth-Dimensional density. Your consciousness must increase in vibrational frequency before you can discuss multidimensional interrelations. I have already told you that all is present in the Here-and-Now. The past and future will become irrelevant accordingly. Nevertheless, you are characterising your future with your past, and the current condition. You will learn to handle this and to create a new level of existence. Move into the new era full of trust. All you need is set up inside you and will develop according to your integrated vibrational amplitude. New Earth is a long evolutionary cycle that you are now joining. It will develop into the "Golden era" and return you to paradise. The next generations to follow will build on your creativity and your potential. You are the pioneers of ascension from darkness into Light.

You have operated in darkness so far. However, Light will more and more point out the entire range of your skills and opportunities to you. Immense variety is disclosed to you, in harmony with the greater whole. That ascension truly is a gate to a new existential level in all matters. Take courage. Let go of the old and walk trustingly into the Light, to meet your destiny.

The human body is developing into the body of Light, your personal Merkabah. You are using it to access and explore the multidimensional space. You are once again connecting to your stellar past. You are returning to your cosmic roots and connecting to All-That-Is. Love is your motivation, your highest asset, your reason for manifestation. Light and Love are your origin and your future into all eternity.

All of creation is made of condensed Light. That includes your bodies. Your souls, your spirits, originate in the source of Light, our god, our goddess. You are Light on a mission. As the vibrational frequency of Light on Earth increases, all matter – including humans – will radiate and the separation from All-That-Is will dissolve. Light connects everything and harmonises opposites. A new clarity will dissolve past issues and offer solution approaches. The increase of the frequency of Light will, therefore, lead you to the new era and transform the negative. Allow those transformations and open yourselves to the Light. Continue trustingly along your path on the spiral of Light, back home.

You have deserved the "Golden Age", or the rediscovered paradise, after your commitment in this dense matter. It is your reward after the effort. Your dedication has anchored Light in the dark times. You have protected and nurtured it and you are now bringing it to shine brightly. The cosmic family thanks you cordially and is yearning to meet you.

The Heart

The heart is your physical engine that distributes your blood in your bodies by pulsations. It is intricately connected to Mother Earth and her own pulsations. Ideally, both of them will vibrate harmoniously and nurture each other. If the heart's frequency is impaired, the connection to Mother Earth may stabilise it. Never forget that you are intricately connected to her. You are not separated from her in any manner. You need each other. That awareness will help you better handle your physical hearts. Just as Earth is nurtured by the cosmic pulsations, so will you. That feeling of being separate from All-That-Is will now come to an end. You will find to your surprise just how strongly everything is connected to everything else. You will change or adjust your lives accordingly. You are a universe of your own, embedded into a greater one. Everything depends on everything else. There is no difference. Everyone and everything has their or its own specific place and function.

That energetic connection to All-That-Is is why the heart is ascribed the quality of love. Love keeps the micro- and macrocosmos together. Love is the energy that makes interaction of creation possible. It is the basic matrix of everything.

Your physical hearts were badly traumatised in the past by pain and suffering. In this time of ascension, you will be shown those wounds so that they can be finally healed. Give your hearts the rest they need, and support them to the best of your abilities. They will lead you into the Fifth Dimension. The energy of the heart is the energy that connects you to All-That-Is. It is the basis of your future activities, no matter if in development of New Earth, in communication among yourselves or with your cosmic siblings. Reason and feelings will merge in your hearts. Strengthened by the energy of love, your thoughts will have integrated demands to your projects and activities.

The energy of the heart will let you build a new society where everyone can unfold. Discrimination of races is no longer part of this new era. Instead, the different races on Earth reflect the different star-born who manifested on Earth. The memory of your cosmic roots will give all humans a new self-worth. They will all provide the abilities of their respective races – their origins – to Earth without reservation. Earth has been visited by many space farers from the very first days. Among other things, they carried along their local favourite plants and animals. That helped bring about the diversity that characterises Earth in her flora and fauna.

Unconditional Love is the cosmic glue that holds everything in the micro- and macrocosmos together. The higher a planet is vibrating, the more conscious its residents will be. The heart and its energy of Love will become the central starting point of all activities and interactions.

Your hearts will be able to better open themselves to that divine energy of Love. The harmonisation of polarities will give them the protection they need to unfold their energy and to let it flow. Your thymus, which is the connection between your physical hearts and your heart chakra, will once again fully perform its function and support you in your divine co-creatorship. The human body is the vessel and expression of divine Love in one. It radiates that energy of Love to nourish its entire environment and influence the whole.

All residents on Earth are now given better access to that divine, unconditional Love. The transformation of your living conditions is unavoidable for this reason. Global social changes will follow. The energy of the heart includes everything. Its influence, for example on your neglected Earth, will bring about great, healing projects that support Earth. That energy of the heart will open you up to cosmic space and break up your former limitations.

Flowing with the Current

The energy that is currently reaching Earth is powerful, demanding stability and courage from humans to entrust themselves to it. Rebelling against it is useless. It would only cost you a lot of strength. That energy is an evolutionary thrust that positively affects Earth and her humans. Do not oppose it, but try to flow with that current as well as you can, and to enjoy it. It will take you to your destination. It will transform your personalities and it will free you from old ballast. As reborn residents of Earth, you will be born into a new octave of existence and create New Earth. A long, dark era will be replaced by a Light-filled one. It is as if you were still caught in a tunnel, but already able to see the sunny exit with all of its clarity and inexhaustible opportunities that are ahead of you. This metaphor is showing the difference between the Old and New Earth quite well. Outside of the tunnel, you will, of course, find entirely different opportunities. Look forward to casting off your limitations and to conquering what is new. The available Light will point out many ways in which you can enjoy your further development. Let the current energetic current lead and guide you. Flow with it with all your senses, and be aware of your cosmic journey with Mother Earth.

Earth, too, flows with the cosmic currents and communicates with her neighbour planets in that manner. The entire solar system is integrated into that process of ascension, expecting a new dimensional octave.

The transformations that Earth and her people are managing are strict and bound to increase until the time of ascension. This is why stability is in the greatest demand in such times. You will not find it on the outside, but only inside yourselves. Your personal connection to Earth and creation, in harmony with rest and stillness in your innermost, will give you the desired stability and feeling of being embedded in All-That-Is. That way, you can meet chaos and constant changes step by step with the necessary distance, to make smart decisions. This evolutionary thrust demands a lot from humans. It will lead you to your responsibility towards yourselves and the whole. You are currently developing your mastery, your initiation into the cosmic family. Such tests are always a challenge. Initiations can only be achieved by prepared initiates, such as mankind is right now. Living on Earth now qualifies you to take that step if you wish.

Free will is the highest law on Earth. Therefore, every human will make a personal decision on how they want to live their lives, and which path they want to choose. There are no chosen. Everyone chooses their own unique path.

Just as Earth knows her seasons, similar cycles exist in cosmic space. Earth has weathered a long winter. The first messengers of spring become evident. Like nature is reborn in spring, so are Earth and her humans now reborn. You have gotten used to winter to the point where the new, awakening season has to shake your basis before you can recognise it. Dear humans. Welcome the new season. Welcome spring. Discover and enjoy it to the fullest. Awaken from your hibernation and welcome the new entity that you are with all of its skills and potential. Your senses were compressed and limited in the past. The new time gives you the opportunity to use and enjoy the entire bandwidth of your senses. A new life is disclosing itself to you, with a new access to creation. Feel All-That-Is and abandon yourselves to this divine instance of life, this cosmic dance. Joy and harmony will accompany you on that new vibrational wave.

The divine fanfares and trumpets will soon reach a conscious mankind and accompany it on its further journey. Earth will radiate and send its message of mastery into the cosmos. Your cosmic siblings will thank you for your strength and your courage to take this evolutionary step, and praise the ONE.

The New Diversity

The increased vibrational frequency will soon enable you to perceive new colours and sounds. The range expands and will give you access to spherical music and the cosmic colour range. Since your senses are developing, you will feel your everyday lives more and more, and your intuition will become part of your lives, a talent that you will now trust in. You will be able to recognise increasingly that your intuition equals information from a superordinate reality with an integrated approach. Through your liberation, you are learning to think in new tracks and to trust in cosmic, multidimensional ideas, and to put them into practice. Those ideas are the basis of your development and the fertile soil of your new lives. The pallet of your options expands exponentially, enabling you to venture into new territories. All matters of human community, technology, and science are beneficiaries of that opening. Great innovations will come and revolutionise life on Earth. The changes to the vibrational density will facilitate handling of matter as well as the ethereal. You will integrate the latter increasingly in your work, and thereby develop a new access to matter. The entire range of energies will be consciously available to you and can be creatively modelled or processed by you. The interrelations will become evident and create clear concepts.

This holistic approach is the key to the new era, avoiding unilateral solution approaches. The implementation of intergrade projects will make you creator gods and creator goddesses in your reality. That way, you are developing a greater understanding and knowledge for the terrestrial, as well as the cosmic interrelations. The more experience you collect, the wiser your decisions and projects will be. This is about feeling a new reality and experimentation with new physical and mental situations. Since diversity on Earth will greatly expand, you will have to learn to manage that flood in all matters. Approach exploration of your new reality step by step, and do not let the new overwhelm you too much. All of these cosmic gifts are due to the high vibrational frequency that Earth takes up. These innovations have always been available to you, but they could not be recognised by you due to the low vibrational frequency. The cosmic abundance belongs to you as well as to your cosmic siblings. It is your cosmic human right that you have had to do without for so long. It is similar to being held imprisoned for a long period of time, and then finally approaching the day of release. Enjoying unrestrained freedom after such a restricted phase is a skill that needs to be acquired first. Even very Light-filled innovations can have their pitfalls, and they need a time of adjustment. Personal integration of the high-vibrational frequency will enable you to do this well, and you will be resonating with what is new. The better you integrate the high vibration into your bodies, the better you will be able to handle the innovations. I would like to emphasise that transformed individuals liberated from old ballast will find it easier to integrate this high vibration. I would, therefore, greatly ask you to take your own mental processes seriously and to liberate yourselves from old, obsolete ballast so that you can fully welcome the new. You are not going into this new era without preparation. You have been prepared for this for a very long time. Your agreement to accompany and support this octave jump is the reason for your current incarnation on Earth. This is a great experience for souls. This leads to development of an incredible wealth of experience that they will share with their cosmic siblings.

All facets of the new diversity will soon be available to you and can be implemented creatively for development of New Earth. You can now plan and implement unconventional projects. The increased vibration of Light will bring you clarity and radiate into hidden angles that you have been unable to perceive before. Your view of things is given a higher perspective that permits an integrated approach.

Even though variety of Old Earth is now reducing, in particular concerning flora and fauna, different species will develop in the new time. They will be better able to deal with the high vibration. Some of your animals have accompanied and supported you for a very long time. They are now slowly leaving Earth in order to settle on their home planets again. Their work for Earth and for mankind is complete. All beings living on Earth are in a symbiotic relationship with her and have their own special order for the whole. Everything is interconnected – from the smallest to the largest. Everyone is contributing to the project Earth and beyond. Through the increase of dimensional quality, everyone will experience integration of the new vibrational frequency along with the accompanying effects.

Humans, as well as flora and fauna, are living beings, and therefore exposed to the same adjustments, everyone in their sphere. Earth as a whole rises into the Fifth Dimension with the corresponding consequences for everyone and everything.

The high Light potential will, however, richly compensate you for all the challenges you had to overcome. The Garden of Eden is ready to receive and rejuvenate you. So may it be.

Dawn

After a very long span of darkness, Earth is now starting into a new day. Night is over and Light begins to brighten up and illuminate Earth. You will recognise the entire range of her treasures and beauties. Immerse yourselves into these new pallets of being and enjoy your beautiful home and hearth with all your senses. Communicate with Earth and learn from her. The newly developed partnership with her will give you great wisdom, stability, and gratitude. In solidarity with her, you will explore the cosmic space and contribute your experiences. A population connected to Earth in harmony can now break through its borders and tackle new, cosmic experiences. The stability that you receive from Earth will enable you to expand the radius of your experiences and integrate new information. Harmony, a heart quality, will take hold of humans. With its Earth-like qualities, mankind will engage in exchange with its cosmic siblings and connect to them. A new chapter of evolutionary history is about to be written. The old insignia are stored in your DNA, your personal library. They will now be supplemented and expanded with new links. Multidimensional strings of your DNA that have long been silent, begin to play their melodies. The high Light frequencies transform your bodies and turn them into vessels and cosmic gates.

Your DNA will be expanded, which means that the ethereal genetic code will be connected to physical and the entire range will be available. Humanity will be reborn as cosmic citizens who can make use of their entire potential. That development does, of course, influence your bodies. Your inborn self-healing forces are reinforced, and you will do all you can to support your bodies, to take their signals seriously and to act accordingly. A general process of rejuvenation will occur and enable you to actively participate in societal activities all the way into old age. Your physiological will develop into Light bodies, and where there is Light, darkness cannot prevail. The harmonisation of polarities will support this process. Healthcare will focus on healthy humans, supporting and strengthening their immune systems. This is an entirely different approach from the one you are used to now. Your rise of consciousness will let you see that you are a universe embedded in a greater universe. You will take responsibility for yourselves and for the greater universe and recognise that all is interlinked with everything. A separation of that structure, as in the case of your disease cancer, will no longer happen, since the separation from All-That-Is will be removed.

The conscious understanding of connection will enter all matters, from the smallest to the largest, of projects. Your responsibility towards the whole will determine all your thoughts and activities. You will become conscious co-creators and try to promote the whole and to continue to ascend on the evolutionary spiral of Light. All cosmic citizens of Light have connected to that game and will try to contribute to the best of their abilities.

The solar mastery that Earth and her residents are now striving for will birth them into a new level of existence that is unknown in their pasts. That is why I keep calling this a rebirth: you will leave the past behind, and new impressions, and a new life, are waiting for you.

This also leads to great adjustment of all matter, and of course also of your bodies. Your current body and wellness culture is intricately connected to that raised vibration. You will notice that your bodies are important. Without them, you cannot manifest yourselves here on Earth. Of course, those bodies should be healthy, in order to better integrate the high Light frequencies. You have unconsciously understood that already. You take care of your nutrition. You try to centre yourselves and to support Mother Earth. Those needs are signs of a higher consciousness. With the energies that are flushed more and more strongly onto Earth, your consciousness will be subject to great growth. It will convert and heal your minds and bodies. The process of birth happens inside every individual, manifesting on the outside only afterwards. You, too, transform in the same manner in which a caterpillar turns into a butterfly. Some will do so more quickly, others more slowly, and yet all of mankind will be affected by it. This will be a global, Earth-spanning process of rebirth for mankind. Those who do not want to submit to the process will depart and continue their learning experiences in a similar vibrational density. Free will is the highest law on Earth. The decision of whether to experience that ascension into the Fifth Dimension or not rests with every individual. The reasons for avoiding this are known by every individual soul. It must, therefore, be respected. Earth and the entire solar system are switching to a higher octave of existence with their willing residents.

A conscious population, combined with the new societal and physical structures, will work wonders on Earth, take care of their planet and travel and explore the cosmos with her. Earth is, in a way, your mothership. She is your home and your hearth. Association to a specific planet with her very specific properties gives the galactic family of Light its incredible diversity. Look forward to getting to know your cosmic siblings and to consciously participate in the cosmic events.

Day is breaking. Light is warming your hearts and pointing you on your future path. That path is characterised by Love. That is a Love of cosmic qualities. Consciousness of the unity with All-That-Is will strongly influence your heart quality and design your manifestations on Earth. Additionally, polarities will be harmonised, and emotional fluctuations balanced out. The level of the heart is, as already mentioned, the quality of your future relationships with yourselves and your environment.

The cosmic frequencies of Light and Love that now reach Earth more strongly, are the information of our creator. Their amplitude has now reached a strength that people can no longer ignore. Your adjustment to those high energy frequencies and their integration into your bodies and into Earth are the reason for your current transformation, both on a private and global level. Soon, vibration will have reached the level of ascension. The time remaining will, therefore, still experience energetic intensification with the corresponding effects for every individual, as well as for the whole. That high vibration of Light and Love will restore the cosmic order on Earth and embed her population once again in All-That-Is. Evolution of mankind will continue on its path of Light.

Its time of separation is over, as is the suffering connected to it. The entry in paradise, however, leads to great personal transformation, the release of old, narrowing value systems and dedication to that high energy. Ascension into the Fifth Dimension is, therefore, not coming to you without effort. It is developed with your will. The choice is yours! You are responsible for your lives and your future path. You know the old and have tried to handle it. The new, however, is like a jump into the void. That takes courage and trust. I have tried to introduce what is new to you. I have tried to explain it and to point out the connections. The choice, however, is with you directly. Everyone must make this decision on their own, and also walk the path alone. This is an initiation into your status of adults, into the higher race of Adam Kadmon, to become cosmic co-creators.

Emanations of the Sun and All-That-Is

Your sun is nourished by the other light carriers in the cosmos, forwarding that information to her planets. Her energy penetrates all matter of the solar system, as well as its ethereal areas. No atom will be left out, no area will be neglected. The cosmic order is a network of all physical and ethereal levels. An action on one level will lead to a reaction that goes deeply into cosmic space. It can impair All-That-Is or raise it up, depending on the sense in which the action is taken. I have told you about your new responsibility, and your status as adults. Since the reaction of your actions affects the whole, you need to take responsibility for the whole. This was difficult for you to understand before, since you were separated from everything. The time of separation will soon be over. You will recognise that everything is connected to everything down to the deepest layers.

Loneliness and solitude are an illusion. Of course, one can, and should, withdraw from everyday life. Nevertheless, you will remain connected to everything. Your thoughts are concerning not only yourselves. They

187

are an energy you emanate and that is taken up by everything. The corresponding reaction will follow. Therefore, take care of your thoughts and be aware of your responsibility.

The increase of gamma radiation of your sun brings clearer information onto Earth that raises the whole into a Fifth-Dimensional density of being. Third- and Fourth-Dimensional structures have dissolved. They are no longer compatible with the high vibration. This will lead to chaos and confusion at first, until the new Fifth-Dimensional laws have been rooted.

This time of transition that you are currently experiencing may be difficult for Earth and her humans. However, it is what returns cosmic order to your planet, and thereby restores her abundance.

Properties of Earth and mankind that have been neglected before will once again take their equal place in the whole. Harmonisation of the polarities goes to the deepest layers of your being, as well as that of Earth. Above and below, inside and outside will be stabilised in the middle, to produce a magnificent radiation. Every atom contributes to ascension of the vibrational frequency. Every atom contains the divine spark of our creator.

Bundling of the high energy creates the new and innovative based on different laws from the dissolved old. The radiance of the new vibrational frequency brightens up all matter, all life on the planet, and the relationships of humans to themselves and between each other. That Light brings transparency into all matters of Earth. This means spiritualisation of All-That-Is! The higher self that has been separated from you so far once again merges with the human body. That part of the divine unity merges with you and transforms man into a divine co-creator. You will once again become the multidimensional beings that you have always been. The high frequencies of Light will bring you back home after a long cycle of separation and splitting.

You have come to know the strong density of matter and are now ready to explore higher-vibrational aspects of matter, to approach and apply new laws. Rejoice, my dear people. Your explorations will astonish you. The simple handling of highly vibrating matter will make your creativity soar. The bundled power of your thoughts will let you support your projects and create new ones. Reunification with All-That-Is will let high energy flow. All is connected and interlinked. Creation is accessible to all beings and will be designed by everyone together. Interaction will bring you incredible innovations and a new understanding of the whole. Your patterns of belief in all areas will be expanded. Old thought structures will collapse. They have no foundations anymore. A new era and a new platform of life is about to develop and will come true very soon.

As you can see, the changes that are in store for you affect all of your areas of activity, your bodies, and your minds. You will be reborn as new beings in full power and strength. Your cosmic siblings are greatly looking forward to contacting you and to enter into a partnership with you. You have been separated from the cosmic family for a long time. Finally, you will embrace each other now. The yearning for a conscious population of the Earth has been great in cosmic space. Finally, the day has come. Gratitude and respect for your ascension work will accompany your admission to your cosmic family. The entire sector of the galaxy is brightened up by your efforts. Your creative and transformative power reaches deeply into space. We all praise the ONE. We are all the ONE. Amen.

As an awakened mankind, you are part of the Galactic Confederation. Together with your cosmic siblings, you will determine its fate. Your invaluable experiences will enrich this community and your mastery will sound deeply into the cosmic space.

Epilogue

My beloveds, I thank you for allowing me to have the privilege to contribute to Earth and her humans in this and other forms. It is and was a great joy for me. I am grateful to have this conscious contact with you. This is a contact that will go beyond these lines. All it takes is your consent. I embrace every reader of this book in my heart. You humans are all loved deeply, as you have been from the very beginning of all time, and as you will be in eternity.

I cordially thank Mother Earth for all the efforts she has taken upon herself in order to enable mankind to make these experiences. With the powerful support of her people and the cosmic forces, her healing process will now accelerate. Her unconditional love, her indulgence and patience, are her unmistakable maternal properties. Her extraordinary beauty not only casts its spell on humans, but also on space farers from the most remote cosmic reaches. Going on this evolutionary jump with Terra is a privilege, a gift to mankind now incarnated.

We are all connected in the ONE in love, and in love we all continue on our paths into the Light, to the SOURCE of us all.

Praised be the bearers of Light. They will create the heavens.

So may it be.

Acknowledgement

My dear niece Melody Aimée Reymond made it possible for me to publish this book in this manner. I thank her wholeheartedly for her commitment, her motivation and her unceasing effort.

Other Books by the Same Author

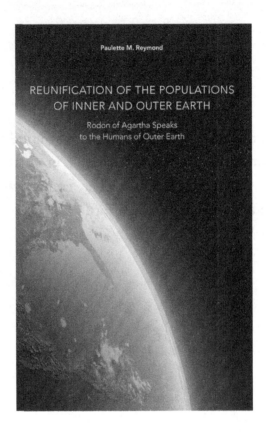

Reunification of the Populations

of Inner and Outer Earth

Rodon of Agartha Speaks to the Humans of Outer Earth

With great joy, my population, the Agarthans of the Inner Earth, has now decided to contact the civilisations of Outer Earth. This will allow them to understand their home planet Earth under a new aspect, and give us the opportunity to introduce ourselves. Millennia of separation from our joint residence on Earth are finally coming to an end. The new, high, Fifth-Dimensional energy will now permit this connection. As a unified population of Earth, we will be able to embrace our cosmic family of Light and contribute to the cosmic Councils.

The time has come to get to know each other and to take care of the fate of our dear Mother Earth together. We are all ONE, residents of Earth, Terra, or Gaia. We travel together with her on our cosmic journey of Light. May our presence bring you joy and show you Terra in a new light.

With great yearning, we await our reunification with our brothers and sisters of Outer Earth.

Alao
Your brother, Rodon of Agartha

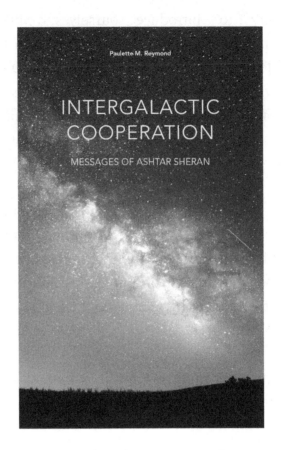

Intergalactic Cooperation

Messages of Ashtar Sheran

I, Ashtar Sheran, have been closely connected to the cosmos in love since its very beginning. It is my task to give Light its place, and to guide and support Earth and her people into this ascension into the Fifth Dimension. Mankind is now ready for this evolutionary leap and to take responsibility for their future. We are all connected in the ONE and welcome the residents of Earth in the galactic family.

In this book, I would like to provide some information that will help you leave behind your island existence and contact your star siblings. Break through your limitations and accept your multi-dimensional heritage! We are all connected to, and interwoven with, each other. We are creating the new Heaven and the new Earth together. Your divine nature will enter even your smallest atom and imbue you with new strength.

Love is the quintessence of all of creation. Without love, the cosmos would dissolve!

Help for Ascension into the 5th Dimension

Messages from Sirius A

Earth and her humans are about to complete a dimensional change. This is why the time in which we are now living on Earth is rich in transformation. The Sirians want to help us humans during this important time of transition. We are equal space siblings. With their brief statements, they aim to specifically reach people who do not have the time to deal more intensely with the subject of dimensional change. These are instructions for a time of pervasive changes.

We all contribute in the Light of the ONE. We are all connected to each other. Love will keep us together forever.

Made in the USA
Coppell, TX
09 October 2024

38441714R00118